Elkie Kammer

Discovering who I am

Growing up in the sensory world of Asperger Syndrome

-an autobiography-

Brandon Press
Inverness/Scotland

© Elkie Kammer 2007

First published in 2007 by
Brandon Press
2 Lodge Road
Inverness, IV2 4NW
Scotland

British Library Cataloguing in Publication Data.
A catalogue record for this book is available
from the British Library.

ISBN 978 0 9554895 0 1

Contents

Preface   5
1) Early Years   8
2) Being part and apart   17
3) Chaos and Order   26
4) Family Breakdown   38
5) Losing Control   47
6) The Nightmare continues   55
7) Dogs and Children   64
8) In Hospital   73
9) On a new Path   85
10) The Quest goes on   94
11) At University   99
12) Someone to meet me where I am   104
13) The Start of a Career   115
14) The Answer   124
Epilogue   130
Recommended Reading   134

4

Preface

I know that it won't take a minute. All I have to do is lift the receiver, dial the number and tell the person at the other end of the line that I cannot come to her party. I should have done it a week ago, when I found her invitation on my answer machine. Since then, the little note has looked at me accusingly, pointing to the telephone and making me feel guilty and stupid. Twice I actually tried it. I lifted the receiver, looked at the number, then put it down again. Why couldn't I just do it? Other people use the phone every day. They even enjoy making phone calls. For me, it always involves a struggle. My body goes rigid and breathing becomes hard. I would have to wait until I feel really brave and even then the questions go round and round in my mind: "Who will be at the other end? Will I recognise the voice? What if I can't make out what they say? Or what if they ask questions which I can't answer straight away? You don't get thinking time on the phone." And so on.

Finally I do it, just to get it over with. I let the phone ring until the answer machine at the other end announces that the person is not available. I could leave a message after the tone. Well, I hadn't really thought about an answer machine, but in a way it makes things easier. No unpredictable comments or questions. I say my name and that I cannot come to the party, then plonk the receiver down. Phew! I have done it. For a moment I am relieved. Then doubt is creeping in. Did I say the right thing? Did I say enough? It took me years to learn that the first thing to say when meeting a person or speaking to someone on the phone should be: "How are you?" I used to always come straight out with the purpose for my call. But I couldn't really ask an answer machine how it felt, could I? Perhaps I should have explained why I wasn't able to come to the party, but that was a problem in itself.

Most people don't understand how difficult I find informal gatherings, especially when they involve a crowd of people, many of whom I don't know. I have never been able to figure out how other people do it, socialise I mean, chat with ease and enjoyment. I can't even understand what someone is saying to me, when there are too many voices all around me. I am hopeless remembering names and faces, even of people I meet every day. I am oblivious to many things which other people use as topics for small talk. Instead, I often find my attention captivated by things which other people don't notice, like the pattern the sun light draws on the carpet or an artificial gum tree in a corner. I might actually feel closer to the gum tree or the carpet than to the people in the room. Only the many voices and noises around me soon become so painful that I want to cover my ears and scream.

Then there is the party food. Most people seem to enjoy a variety of exotic dishes to pick and mix. I don't. I like to eat the same simple food every day, from the same dish and at the same time. I use the same pan to boil my potatoes and vegetables and throw a "lost" egg in at the end. This has been my dinner for most of my life. It is easy to chew and to swallow and to digest, and my body knows what to expect.

And then there is my evening routine before I go to bed. Parties tend to last well into the night. I cannot cope with late nights. When I am tired it is even harder to function like "normal" people than it is when I am fresh and alert. Half past nine is usually my threshold when I start going through my evening rituals – shower, physio exercises, a cup of herbal tea, saying my prayers and slipping into my imaginary world – so that by eleven o'clock I drop off to sleep.

Just as well I got the answer machine. Maybe it was worthwhile waiting. I sigh. Why does life have to be so complicated? Or is it me who is complicated? I don't know. I only know that it is useless to fight against myself or to try to be who I am not. On the contrary, the more I have learned to understand and to accept myself, the better equipped I am to find understanding and acceptance from others and to find my place in this world.

Chapter 1: Early Years

I was born in the 1960s in the north of Germany as the third child of what would later be four. My parents came from the East and had therefore very little material resources. In fact, my father had just embarked on a postgraduate degree in mathematics and information technology (then in its infancy) and my mother was trying to make ends meet in a tiny attic flat with three little children, all still in nappies which had to be washed in a big cauldron on top of the coal fire stove. She often went hungry to ensure that her husband and children were fed, and she suffered from tetany fits due to calcium deficiency. This was especially bad during and after her pregnancy with me, and I later experienced similar fits.

I wasn't planned, but in those days before the invention of contraception babies just happened, unless one was blessed with a very understanding and self-controlled husband. Because our attic flat was so small and crowded, we spent a considerable time in our "canvas lodge" at the seaside, first in Holland, which was only a stone's throw away, and later at the Baltic Sea. There we had the freedom to dig in the sand, splash in the waves and roll down the dunes all day long. According to my mother, these were the happiest days she remembers with us, "the days before I lost you", she once told me in a letter. Even so, it wasn't easy for her, knitting our clothes as it was cheaper than buying them, cooking over a camping stove and using the public facilities of the campsite, whilst still suffering from occasional fits of tetany.

So at the age of seven months, I was bundled off to my Latvian grandmother and cousins (then living in a village north-east of Frankfurt), where a month later I took my first unaided steps. I certainly wasn't clumsy, although, having been born two weeks overdue, I was heavier built than my siblings. On my first birthday, so I am told, I climbed over the playground fence, but somehow my jumper got caught and I dangled upside down on the other side until I was rescued. By then I was back with my own family. I learned a lot by watching my older sisters who were a close-knit pair, though a year and a half apart, and occasionally let me join in their games. However, my second sister could be quite cruel or simply careless at times, and after she once almost suffocated me, my mother did not let us play together unsupervised anymore.

When I was about 18 months old, I got lost in the town where we lived. Once more I had climbed over the playground fence, this time successfully, and just went exploring. By the time my absence was noticed, I was well out of sight. My mother and several neighbours went in search of me. They even called the police out after a while. Three hours later I turned up again, seemingly unharmed and not unduly distressed, though nobody knows where I had been all that time and I was too young to tell them.

It wasn't the only time that I got lost. It happened again on the beach, when I accidentally missed our tent and walked on and on in search of it, until some kind person picked me up and brought me back. This time I was distressed and I soon developed a fear of getting lost which made me rather clingy. My sense of direction has never been good, and I am glad I learned map reading at an early age or else I would have walked off the edge of the planet by now.

The other fear I developed during the first couple of years of my life was the fear of sudden noises. If I saw a tractor or lorry coming towards us on the road, I would put my hands over my ears until it had passed. Every time my mother wanted to use the food mixer or the vacuum cleaner, she made sure that she put me out on the balcony first with the door closed behind me to avoid unnecessary upset. In fact, sounds have always had a profound effect on me. They don't just elicit thoughts and emotions, but physical sensations as well. I could always pick up a lot more sounds than most people around me, which later led to a thorough examination of my ears, but no medical cause was found.

When I was two years old, I suddenly became very ill with a mysterious stomach bug. For a whole month I refused to eat and my parents had great difficulty forcing enough liquid down my throat to keep me from dehydration. In the end they were ready to take me to hospital to be put on tubes, although my mother resented the idea. However, at that point I must have reached the bottom line of the illness and began to perk up. I had lost a lot of weight, and from the chubby baby emerged a skinny toddler. Ever since then I had to be careful with food, which in those days wasn't too difficult as we had a very basic diet and I was never keen on new tastes anyway.

According to my parents, I had no problem acquiring speech. As in so many other ways, I just copied my older sisters and had lengthy conversations with my dolls. There was no question as to imaginative play. I spent most of my waking hours in my own little world, making up stories or imitating what I saw around me. I usually preferred to play on my own, as nobody could alter my story line and move it into an undesired direction. Also, my second sister, perhaps out of low self-esteem or jealousy often taunted me and looked for ways to belittle me.

My very first memory is of the toilet block at the campsite by the Baltic Sea. Water closets hadn't reached that part of the world yet. Instead, we had something called "thunder logs", a wooden box with a hole to sit on. One of these boxes had two holes, a two-seater-toilet, which was my sisters' favourite, as they could sit there together and chat away until business was done. I remember sitting on the one-seater with both my sisters next door chatting and laughing and my second sister making fun of me, while I felt stupid and hurt. I reckon, I was about three years old at the time.

Another memory connected with those toilets comes to my mind. Now and again a big tanker would arrive to pump out the faeces. On one such occasion I was watching from a safe distance, desperate to use the toilet and yet terrified of the noisy machine. I still remember thinking: "Where can I go now?" But somehow I didn't make the connection with the potty we always kept in the tent for the night. Well, after all it wasn't night time.

The summer before my third birthday, we practically lived in our "canvas lodge" for good. My father was finishing his studies and applying for jobs, while my mother expected another baby. Her younger sister, who was also a student at that time, spent most of her holidays with us to help her. She once rescued me out of a swamp I had fallen into while exploring a new area with my sisters. It didn't deter me from further explorations, though. Like climbing the fence on my first birthday, it only served to ignite a spark for fresh adventures.

My mother remembers me riding on her hip through the waves of the Baltic Sea, returning her smile and singing together. I have no memory of this and I know from later experience that my mother often interpreted my reactions in different ways from what I felt. So it may well be that even at that point I wasn't too keen on skin to skin contact. As autumn approached and the sea became rougher and colder and the baby in her womb grew bigger, her smiles and singing gave way to worries. My father had finally found a job in West Berlin, but he couldn't find affordable accommodation for a family of six. Shortly before my brother was born in November, he finally came across something suitable: the ground floor flat of an old hunting lodge in the village of Rudow on the south-east tip of West Berlin. It came with a big garden and an old dog and the owners, an elderly couple, lived upstairs. The flat consisted of a kitchen, a bathroom and a large hall, which my parents divided into chambers by using wardrobes and curtains. My sisters shared a little chamber with a bunk bed in it and I had a smaller chamber to myself. My brother's cot would be placed in my parents' "bedroom", while the ancient dog slept in front of the fire where one day she didn't wake up.

I must have felt very confused with so many changes happening at once, for I started to wet my bed again and became quite anxious, especially at night. Waking up in the dark, I would feel my way to my parents' bed, but there was no room for me with the baby huddled in my mother's arms. A few times I managed to squeeze in at the edge, only to fall out as soon as I was asleep. So I resolved that it was better to stay in my own bed. I would lie awake for what seemed like hours, feeling sad and lonely and frightened. During the day it wasn't much better. I hated to see my little brother drinking at my mother's breast. Why had she replaced me with this new baby? At the same time I sensed how tired and overworked my mother was and that I had better not demand anything from her. My father worked very long hours and his clothes needed to be immaculate which, having little money, meant even more work for my mother.

My sisters started Kindergarten and seemed to be very happy there, learning new songs and games every day. In a way, it widened the gap between us, but it also gave me peace and space to withdraw into my own world and not to be disturbed until they came home at lunch time. The afternoon I would often spend in a conflict. Part of me wanted to join in my sisters' new games and adventures, while the other part couldn't cope with adapting to their ideas. I also became increasingly aware of the difference between myself and them and their friends. While they all seemed to enjoy the discussions and quarrels of playing together, it usually caused me more stress than fun. I easily grew frustrated when others didn't see things the way I saw them or when they spoiled the story line which appeared so clear to me. Again and again I would leave the scene after such confrontations and rather play on my own.

To my mother, this is the time when she "lost" me. She was aware that I needed her help to come to terms with my brother's birth, but she had so little time and strength to spare, and since I withdrew rather than show my emotions openly, it was easier for her to just let me be. But she remembers that I became very quiet and no longer enjoyed physical contact with her. Also, I grew more and more apprehensive about meeting other people, as their questions and interactions caused me a lot of stress. I do remember a few such incidents. Once we went upstairs to say thank you for some food the lady had given to my mother. She tried to make contact with me by telling me some little joke about a meatball, but I was too fascinated by the two rhyming words she used to get the meaning of what she was saying. I couldn't make sense of her attempt to befriend me and felt very confused, knowing that I was somehow expected to respond, but not having a clue as to how. At other times it was a single statement or sentence that caught my attention or even the accent or the hair of a person, so that the rest of the conversation went right past me. This made meeting unfamiliar people very stressful for me and I often hid behind my mother or my siblings to avoid being noticed.

When I was four years old, my mother enrolled me at the Kindergarten which my second sister was still attending, while my oldest sister had just started school. For three consecutive days she left me there, sitting on a bench in the cloakroom, refusing to take my jacket and shoes off and to venture any further. When she came back for me three hours later, I was still sitting there. No amount of coaxing from the teachers and the other children, no promises or threats, nothing would make me let go of that bench. I made it very clear that I wasn't going into that dreadful place full of noisy children and the chaotic jumble of bright toys. So on the fourth day my mother decided to keep me at home. After all, I was rarely getting in her way, since I usually played quietly by myself.

Most of my play was imaginative, often involving my dolls or my little farm set or a purse with toy money which I had been given. I incorporated in my play what I saw and experienced around me as well as inner conflicts and pieces of stories which my mother told us at bedtime. However, I also liked sorting-games or simply to sort my toys and arrange them in front of me: a row of dolls or a row of animals or a row of coins. In the same way, I also enjoyed tidying up. In my little chamber everything had its exact place and I couldn't bear it to be otherwise, as it would make me feel disoriented and lost. Later, when my mother became involved in campaigning against the Vietnam War, my dolls always died at the end and were neatly buried at the bottom of my wardrobe where they stayed until I wanted to play with them again.

Outside I enjoyed digging in the sandpit, climbing trees, pretending to be hunting rabbits or sailing a ship and building all sorts of constructions with sticks and stones and whatever I found in the garden. I am sure that at that stage nobody had any concerns about my mental state. I was a "loner", yes, but every generation has seen people who didn't quite fit in with the norm. Only my mother was wondering now and again if I was really as contented with myself as it appeared. Perhaps I did need help to become more part of the family, but by then I had become such a stranger to her that she didn't know what to do.

Chapter 2: Being Part and Apart

Shortly before my sixth birthday I started school. I was already able to read, as I had taught myself with my sisters' school books. Unlike Kindergarten, school was compulsory, but it was also more formal and structured which helped me settle in. We were forty children in the class, seated in long rows facing the blackboard, as was common in those days. As far as I remember, the only other items in the classroom were a storage cupboard, a world map and a clock. The windows looked out across the playground and behind it lay a dense forest. As calm as the visual environment, so was the audio one, since we had a very strict teacher for the first three years who didn't tolerate any nonsense during lesson time. She had very clear rules and stuck by them.

Outside the village was a disused brick factory which served as temporary housing for homeless families. The children who came from the factory were extremely rough. I guess, this was necessary in order to survive in their environment. However, a lot of them were also very cruel, probably treating others the way they were treated at home. The majority of children in my class came from families who had lived and worked in Rudow for several generations or whose parents commuted to the city for work.

Right from day one I had difficulty understanding the pupils in my class. Unlike my sisters, who had mixed with them since our arrival in Rudow, I was not tuned in to the nuances of their accent, and the fact that most of them didn't speak clearly at all made it even harder for me to decode their speech. My parents and relatives had always talked to us in a rather academic High German and that was the language I understood and used. Also, it would drive me mad when people used wrong grammar, as to me it contorted the flow of language and hurt my ears. It didn't occur to me that other people were used to a different way of speaking, but what would alienate me even more from my class mates was the fact that I was thinking on a completely different wavelength.

Those early seventies were the years of Che Guevara and the Liberation Wars in Latin America. They were the years of the Vietnam War and the first nuclear power stations. They were also the years of the student revolts, the hippies and the women's rights movement, which was all part of my mother's world. For my father, these were the years of new advances in information technology and data processing, the invention of artificial intelligence, of micro chips and new global connections. In our family no thought was given to pop stars and Olympic heroes, the latest fashion or variations of hopscotch, and so I had no interest in it. In the same way that I felt upset when people used incorrect grammar, it would make me angry to hear others go overboard in their adoration for a singer or a footballer. If there was one singer worthy to be adored, then it was Victor Jara in Chile who was persecuted by the dictator for his political ideals. Together with others like himself, he was herded into the Olympic Stadium in Santiago, where he was still singing and playing his guitar until the soldiers cut his fingers off. Instead of crying out in rage and pain, he kept on singing, still smiling when the bullet went through his head, as he knew that he had nothing to regret. Thus were our heroes at home.

To a certain extend, I was probably the most intolerant pupil in our class, but to me it looked as if everybody else was wrong. The lessons themselves were not too bad, although I often felt bored when the teacher explained something several times which I had understood the first time round, especially in mathematics. I didn't tend to volunteer contributions, but when asked directly, I was able to give the right answers. This earned me the comment on every report card: "not realising her full potential".

I mentioned earlier that this teacher had very strict rules for classroom behaviour, one of which was not to go out to the toilet. After each lesson of 45 minutes we had a short break during which we were allowed to go out and relieve ourselves. As for me, I would hardly ever dare to enter the girls' toilets. Being one of the few unsupervised corners in school, they were a perfect place for bullying. Once I lost half of my scalp to a girl who wouldn't let go of my hair and another time someone deliberately slammed a door into my face, almost knocking my eye out. So instead of going to the toilet block, I relieved myself in the woods behind the playground, where according to the other children the janitor's fierce Alsatian was roaming. The Alsatian didn't sound half as dangerous to me as those human brutes.

However, one particular morning, when the boys had gone to their woodwork lesson and we girls were sewing clothes for our dolls, my bladder suddenly signalled that it was full. I couldn't read the clock yet, so I was just hoping that the lesson would soon be over. After a while my tummy began to ache and I knew that I couldn't hold on for much longer. I was in a real dilemma. Never in my life had I broken a classroom rule. It was simply wrong to do so. But it was also wrong to wet my pants, especially in school. What was I to do? I fought an internal battle until the teacher, noticing my discomfort, asked me what was the matter. Instead of answering, I suddenly broke out in tears and at the same moment I felt the warm liquid run down my legs. What happened next has escaped my memory. In retrospect it just shows me how inflexible my understanding of rules and regulations was.

The playground wasn't the safest place either. I didn't understand other children's games and couldn't see a purpose in them. So I was often wandering around on my own, easy prey for the bullies. One day I strolled over to Matthew, a boy of my own age, whose family was known to me. He was reading some kind of RSPCA magazine and shared it with me. This was something I could relate to and from then on we spent many a playtime together, studying and discussing these poor animals.

When school was out at half past twelve, I didn't wait for my sisters. They very rarely walked home with me, preferring each other's company or that of their friends. In order to escape the bullies, I had the habit of waving to my imaginary granny, before I would run off, calling: "I'm coming, Gran!" It certainly saved me from more black eyes and torn scalps.

A few months after I started school, we moved again. My parents acquired a plot of land about 3 km west of the village and built a house. We all helped to finish it. I remember filling my little wheelbarrow with sand again and again, until the big pile had disappeared and the garden was nice and even. Long after our move, my mother was still busy decorating walls and laying tiles in the kitchen and bathroom. Although my father was finally earning a good salary, money was still scarce, as every penny was needed to pay off the mortgage.

The way to school was now quite long. Since there was no bus and we had no car, we were expected to walk. My sisters soon had bicycles, which left me walking on my own. I rather enjoyed the 45 minutes it took me every morning and every lunch time, walking past the fields and through the forest. In fact, I didn't feel alone. Right beside me walked my angel Cari who was always there for me. I don't know when she first appeared, but for many years she never failed me. I could talk to her about everything and, in contrast to human beings, she was always understanding.

One day my father returned from one of his business trips with a parcel under his arm. He had hardly lifted the lid, when out jumped a white fluffy puppy.

Arthos, the Hungarian sheepdog, became my most important friend. He made up for the human friends I did not have and especially for the lack of physical contact. While it was often even too much for me to shake hands with people without feeling "burned", I enjoyed hugging Arthos, being licked all over and rolling around in the grass with him. Somehow his clumsy movements and his fluffy fur didn't feel threatening to me like human touch. Other animals came and went – cats, rabbits, guinea-pigs and a tortoise and finally my oldest sister's pony, but Arthos was by far my favourite. He was always overjoyed when we came home from school, knowing that now our adventures would start.

Homework was usually done quickly and for the rest of the afternoon we would roam the forest, swim in the lake, cool ourselves under the street pump or poke little holes in the famous wall to spy on the soldiers who were guarding the East German territory. I soon became an expert in climbing the tall fruit trees in our garden. We had races, holding a stop watch to see who was fastest to get to the top, and I loved swinging from branch to branch like a monkey. Soon we got bored with the trees and climbed the walls of the house instead, finding holds for our bare toes and fingers in the tiniest cracks and hauling ourselves right up to the top of the roof. Three children who lived nearby often joined us in these games. It was the only time that I vaguely felt part of a group, as I could make sense of what we were doing and excelled with my agility and complete fearlessness of heights.

In winter we went skiing by tying planks of wood under our boots and using dead branches to steady ourselves with. Or we skidded along the frozen stream until one of us would break in and had to be rescued before the ice closed again. We were out in every weather and it didn't seem to harm us. However, there were many times when the company of the others became too much for me, especially, as I mentioned before, when the storyline of our adventures took on a path which I hadn't expected and which didn't seem logical to me. Then I preferred to withdraw, often to the annoyance of the others, to carry on my own version. I never understood why it made them angry, though. After all, I wasn't interfering, just leaving them to their own devices. In the same way, I didn't understand the children at school who took offence at me for not joining their games or conversations. What harm did I cause them by going my own ways? Did they perhaps feel challenged?

There was one other area in which I could link up with people, and that was through music. My parents were very musical, both playing the old piano which dominated our living room. My sisters and I learned to play the descant recorder as soon as we started school. It didn't take us long to be able to play duets and rounds together, and by the age of eight, I played concertos on the treble recorder, accompanied by piano. I also sang in the school choir. I always loved the fact that each instrument or voice had a different part and yet, together they made up a harmony of sound. Music seemed to have a language of its own without the subtle nuances of other communication which I had so much difficulty to understand. It also had clear mathematical rules, and like maths it was very logical, and as long as everybody kept to their part, it always made a whole.

Maths at school I soon found rather boring, as we didn't move on quickly enough for me. So my brain sought other ways to engage with maths which sometimes almost became an obsession. I still remember looking at the rectangle of my bedroom window and trying to find the length of the diagonal with only the measurements of the frame. It took me several weeks to ponder all sorts of possibilities before I finally came up with a formula that worked. Overjoyed with my discovery, I tried it out on all the rectangles I could find until my enthusiasm wore off.

Maths also played a role in other everyday aspects. For example, each of us had a little jam jar which at the beginning of the week my mother would fill with penny-sweets. My brother and sisters usually ate theirs during the first couple of days and had nothing left for the rest of the week, whereas I laid my sweets out in seven equal piles, counting how many I was to have each day, and I made sure not to eat what belonged to another day. Once my sisters found out what I was doing, they started to beg from me when their own sweets were gone, or even to steal some of mine until I resolved to hide them. Indignantly, they called me a selfish hamster, while I told them they were stupid not to make their stock last for the whole week.

During school holidays we were often sent to different relatives to give my mother a break. I liked to stay with my mother's parents in Frankfurt. My granny had been a teacher for children with special needs until she retired. She was always clear and consistent in her expectations on me, while also being good natured and warm hearted. My grandfather was different. I was scared of him and kept out of his way. He had been shell-shocked during the war, and although he recovered sufficiently to carry on with his job at the bank, in his own home he was often unpredictable. Out of a sudden, he would slap me across the face just because I stood in his way or didn't sit straight at the table or for no apparent reason at all. So I was always happiest when my granny took me out, either on her own or with her local Ramblers Club. I never tired of roaming the forest, searching for some old well or castle ruin or the remains of a Roman Fort, and I loved the smells and the sounds of the woods.

My granny was also one of the best storytellers, and I will never forget our picnics of sandwiches and peppermint tea, sitting on a log and enjoying wide views across the hills and glens. I loved my granny. I even let her hug and kiss me, although I cringed a bit. Whenever I smell camphor oil, which she used on her body, I am flooded by a feeling of warmth.

Chapter 3: Chaos and Order

In my fourth year at school, we got a new teacher. I don't know if our previous one retired or just took another class, but the new teacher was a lot younger and he was a man. He also had quite different ideas about education, and the first thing he did was to turn the classroom upside down. I was shocked when I came back after the summer holidays to find that our orderly rows of desks and chairs had given way to little huddles of group tables. We were to sit anywhere, boys and girls together (though they never mixed voluntarily), and some children had to crane their neck in order to see the blackboard.

Not enough with that, but the white washed walls with their soothing patterns of stone and paint had been covered with all kinds of pictures and words, screaming at us from every side. It took me several weeks just to get used to this new environment, but to the teacher and his teaching style I never got used that year. Suddenly the rules we had lived by for three years didn't count anymore. Pupils were talking to each other and getting up in the middle of the lesson or shouting out without even putting their hand up, and all this obviously under the approval of the teacher.

He also loved practical demonstrations. Once he took us out into the playground to explain how a weather cock works. Only with 40 pupils in the class it was impossible for everyone to get even a glimpse of the object. As I didn't like to be touched and easily panicked in crowds, I stood at the outside of the circle where I could neither see, nor hear what the teacher explained.

Group work was another new item on the agenda. Instead of working quietly on our own as before, we were suddenly encouraged to share ideas with the other children at our table and reach conclusions together. This caused me a lot of problems. First of all, the amount of voices competing with each other made it impossible for me to follow any conversation. Secondly, even if I had something to contribute to a discussion, my line of thought was usually so different from everybody else's and my way of reasoning was too complicated for them, so that my ideas were either ignored or criticised, which drove me further away from my class mates. In order to survive these group discussions and the general noise around me, I soon devised a way of cutting myself off from my surroundings. I would concentrate on a quiet spot, like a floor tile or a vane on my hand, and hum a simple repetitive tune to myself whilst rocking my body to its rhythm. This, at least, calmed me sufficiently to cope with the chaos around me. However, it is needless to say that I learned nothing of what we were supposed to take from these lessons. If it hadn't been for the educational books and games we had at home, I would have intellectually starved that year, while at the same time using all my energy at school simply to prevent a break down. Fortunately, my parents soon realised that I couldn't learn in this setting, and after an assessment by the Educational Psychologist, I was given a place in the district's special unit for able pupils as from P5.

A couple of years earlier, my mother had become friends with my oldest sister's teacher, who in turn introduced her to a group of young teachers and students. They more and more frequently called at our house and soon became "part of the family". I remember some of them helping us to build a tree house and a stable for my sister's pony. They also towed an old car into our garden which we painted with all kinds of pictures. My brother loved to sit in the driver's seat, hardly able to lift his head above the steering wheel, going on long journeys to foreign lands. They brought their guitars and we sat around the campfire singing Communist songs, while roasting potatoes in the ashes and bread over the flames. We gave them circus shows, presenting our latest tricks, like 5 children on one bicycle or walking a tight rope between two trees or poor Arthos being chased through hoola-hoop-rings.

Those are my happy memories of them, but there was also a downside to it. For me it was mainly the insecurity of never knowing who would be at home. At times, our house was full of people, movements and voices, and I had to escape to the stable or the tree house or even further into the woods. They also had heated discussions which frightened me. They would be shouting and swearing at each other and at the end call it a good time. Much of their discussions were about politics and whether to choose a peaceful or a violent response to injustice and environmental exploitation. My mother, having suffered so badly as a young child in and after the Second World War, always insisted on a peaceful approach. She soon became involved in a charity helping street children in South America and war orphans from Vietnam. She also rallied against unfair trade, exploitation of women and environmental destruction and got involved in many petitions, fundraising activities and demonstrations.

For us children, the hunger in the world and the war in Vietnam were an ever present reality with the stories we heard and the pictures we saw through my mother's involvement with the charity. I so much identified with a boy who had lost the power of his legs when he was hit by shrapnel, that for several months I was dragging myself around on crutches for about an hour each day. Most of my dolls soon had arms and legs missing and red felt-tip scratches on their face, being marked by the war. As mentioned earlier, they always died when I had played enough with them and were buried neatly at the bottom of my wardrobe. Death didn't hold any fears for me. It was rather a clean way to finish life.

In the same way in which I identified with the Vietnamese boy, I slipped into the role of other people I heard or read about. One of my favourite characters from a book was Blue Bird, a Red Indian boy. I became this boy, making myself a bow and a quiver with arrows and stealing away barefooted or on the bare back of my sister's pony to hunt rabbits and deer. In the Red Indian fashion, I wore nothing but a loin cloth and an old piece of material around my head with a feather sticking out. When I came across a dead rabbit or mole, I picked it up and carried it home as my prey. Once, while thus stalking through the woods, I suddenly came across a couple of people who, for whatever reason, asked me if I was a boy or a girl. "A boy, of course!" I answered indignantly and it wasn't a lie. At that moment I was Blue Bird, the Red Indian boy. Many years later my mother told me that some neighbours complained to her when at the age of 12 I was still walking about half-naked. However, to me there was nothing wrong about it, since that was what Red Indian boys were wearing.

Clothes were actually a big issue for me, but not in the same way as for other children. To me, the most important aspect of clothing has always been their feel. They have to be as unobtrusive to my skin as possible. I could never wear anything tight without feeling suffocated. This would cause me huge problems later in my teens when my breasts developed. I would rather wear woollen jumpers in the heat of summer to cover this up than to endure the suffocating feeling of a bra. My oldest sister finally saved me by making tops out of vests before they arrived on the market. However, at times I even have a problem wearing them, and as soon as I am on my own, I rip them off to free my body from their intolerable pressure.

All my life I have worn loose trousers, T-shirts and jumpers. I was never keen on jeans, as they are too stiff, and I generally prefer clothes which have already been worn. When my mother started to volunteer with the charity, we soon received bags of second-hand-clothes. Before she passed them on, we could choose what we needed. This was just right for me, whereas my second sister always hated to walk about in other people's cast-offs.

Once I got used to the feel of an item of clothing, I didn't want to take it off again. It had become part of my body. I never forget when my mother threw a pair of trousers in the bin while I was at school. Although more holes than material, they were still my favourite trousers. It had been hard enough to accept that I could no longer wear them to school, but at least they were waiting for me when I came home. Not that day, though, because the rubbish had been collected and my trousers were gone. For several days I was grief-stricken, before I finally adopted another pair of favourites.

It was a similar matter with jumpers. For my 6th or 7th birthday, my mother had knitted me a lovely woollen jumper which I called my "Mami-jumper" and wore day and night. As I grew, my mother had to lengthen the sleeves until it finally became obvious that it didn't fit me anymore. However, by then I had found a cardigan which looked quite different, but felt the same. So I was able to gradually replace it. Up to this day, I find it hard to detach myself from clothes which have become part of my body (my "fur", as my

31

cousin used to call it), and I usually buy my clothes in charity shops to avoid the stiffness of new garments.

Sometimes I even find it hard to put on clothes which have been freshly washed and ironed. Perhaps I could compare the feeling to being clad in a knight's armour or wrapped in sackcloth. It physically hurts. It can even cause me to panic when it seems to deprive me of the vital flow of air. Labels and seams have a tendency to scratch me, so that I remove them or wear underclothes inside out. And then there are certain materials, like nylon, which set my skin "on fire". They are simply impossible for me to wear. At school, other pupils often made fun of the way I dressed, but I learned to shrug their comments off. After all, I had to survive.

My new school was in the city, which meant a 2km walk to the nearest train station, 20 minutes on the underground and another 10 minutes walk to school. We were only about 25 children in the class, and the tables were arranged in a kind of horseshoe with some in the middle facing the blackboard. There were few distractions in the room, but the windows looked out onto the road which at times could be quite busy. The only pupil known to me was Matthew, the animal protector, but I soon realised that I had many things in common with all my new classmates. We had all been selected from different schools within the district because we didn't fit into the mainstream system. None of us had been working to their full potential, and in one way or another we had all been outcasts.

The first thing I noticed about these children was their way of thinking which was much more on my own wavelength. I could discuss with them the dangers of nuclear power stations or the injustice of unfair world trade and I would find most of them interested and knowledgeable in these subjects. On the other hand, if someone disagreed with my opinion and saw things from a different point of view, I felt easily confused and withdrew until I had sorted things out in my own mind and put my world back in order.

The teaching style was different, too. I had never been good at rote learning. In fact, even with the greatest effort I couldn't memorise a single poem. In order to learn about things, I had to understand how they worked. I had to find out for myself. This was just what we were doing now, especially in maths. We were given a problem and had to figure out a solution for it, then test it on various other number combinations to verify our approach. It was exactly what I had always been doing on my own, only for the first time it was rewarded at school.

Latin was one of my favourite subjects, because its grammar was so clear and logical. However, the only way to learn the vocabulary was to form a picture for each word or phrase in my mind. Often I knew exactly where to find a certain word in my vocabulary book, but I had forgotten the picture and so I couldn't translate it. Fortunately, our Latin teacher was very compassionate and never put us under pressure.

Another way to compensate for my bad memory had always been to think in colours. In my mind, every letter of the alphabet has a specific colour and so have the days of the week and the months of the year. I often associate subjects with colours and even places and people. It was also a great help to carry a time table with me and to keep a homework diary in which I would tick what I had finished.

The one subject I was never good at was P.E., despite the fact that I won medals for cross country running. Gymnastic activities really posed no problems for me, as I could climb up a rope in a few seconds and jump on a horse while it was running. However, I could not jump over the box while the teacher was standing beside it with her hands ready to catch me. Neither could I do anything that involved a partner or even the slightest possibility of coming in direct contact with someone else's body. Of cause, I couldn't explain this, as I didn't understand it myself. I only knew that touching people's skin was like touching fire. Why the others didn't feel the same was a mystery to me.

Ball games were another source of much teasing and frustration. I hated being hit by a ball, and so I made sure to keep well out of its way. Since the rules of most ball games were too complicated for me to remember and I didn't like the moral implications of playing against another team, I was always the last one to be picked. However, this was different in athletics, when all I had to do was run as fast or jump as high as I could – and I could outrun and outjump almost everybody of my age.

I had a rather compulsive quest for knowing the reason behind the things we were learning, and if something appeared meaningless to me, I could be extremely stubborn in resisting it. One day, our needle work teacher wanted us to learn how to crochet a kind of oven glove. I insisted that we had no need for oven gloves at home, as we just used our sleeves or a towel, and I didn't want to crochet anything else either. The teacher seemed more amused than offended and asked me what I would like to do instead. I wanted to learn how to mend socks. I only wore hand-knitted socks, and my mother was forever complaining about me getting holes in them. So the teacher had me bring some socks in from home and showed me how to mend them, while all the other girls made their oven gloves.

At home, my mother struggled more and more to preserve some kind of order. As my sisters grew older, they often brought friends home. My brother, too, had his playmates from Kindergarten and later from school, and my mother's friends themselves were coming and going freely as if it was their house. I know that my father occasionally suffered from this chaos, but his work always took him away for many days, sometimes weeks, at a time, and my mother needed the company of other adults, not just her children. As for me, I have already mentioned that at times I had to flee from the noise and the general hustle-bustle at home. The other contrast to the chaos in the house was my little bedroom. Everything had its exact place. Once I finished playing with a certain toy or musical instrument, I returned it to its allocated place to restore order. I found it extremely upsetting when my brother or sisters took something from my room and either didn't bring it back or put it in the wrong place. Similarly I was heartbroken if I couldn't have the same basic food every day. Once we ran out of bread and my mother kindly offered us fried potatoes for supper. However, potatoes were eaten at dinner time and not at night, and I refused to eat them. Instead, for several months I made sure I always kept a hunk of bread in my bedroom in case we ever ran out of it again.

There were other rituals which I had to observe all the time, like turning clockwise when I had turned anti-clockwise or drying the left side of my body before drying the right side. Not obeying these self-inflicted rules, upset the order of my life and filled me with enormous fear.

The other problem I had to live with throughout my childhood and adult life was the difficulty to sleep. I would usually fall asleep all right whilst playing with my soft toys in my bed, but I always woke up a few hours later to go to the toilet. After that I usually lay awake for what felt like hours. Sometimes I got up to look out of the window into the night sky, and I remember that on one such occasion I was sure I saw a rocket land on the moon. Well, up to this day, nobody has believed me. Anyway, rocket or no rocket, I always felt very lonely and asked myself again and again what life was all about. Although we had no religious education, I was always sure that there was Someone behind the universe and that this Being must have got some reason for putting us here.

Chapter 4: Family Breakdown

I don't know how old I was, when my little brother threw away one of his soft toys, an elephant with a stuck ear. My mother rescued it and explained to him that the poor animal was very sad because he didn't want to play with it. The reason why I remember this scene so well is that I felt such deep empathy for the elephant that I could actually hear it cry. I offered to take care of it and to play with it. Later, my brother wanted it back, which was all right with me. I reckon that every child up to a certain age relates to their soft toys and even to other objects in this way, identifying with their perceived feelings. The thing is, I never grew out of it. In fact, it became a big problem for me, and whenever I was asked by psychiatrists about the onset of it, I could only answer that I had always felt like this.

Just before my 12th birthday, our whole class left the Primary School which had hosted us for two years and went to a nearby Secondary Grammar School. However, we still stayed together as a class for all subjects and had our own room in which most of the lessons were delivered.

At the age of 10, I had started to play the cello and was soon invited into several orchestras. I enjoyed the rehearsals and concerts, but avoided the parties and other informal gatherings. I was scared of not knowing what to do on such occasions and how to socialise. Small misunderstandings, which obsessively plagued my mind for weeks afterwards, added to my discomfort and fears. Nevertheless, I had a couple of friends in those days with whom I sometimes even met in private. One was a girl who played the violin and also had a dog. So we occasionally met in each other's house to practise some music together and walk our dogs afterwards. The other friend was one of my class mates who admired my fearlessness in adventurous activities and in standing up for my beliefs. She soon found out that I wasn't as fearless in other areas of life, but she faithfully stayed at my side until I left school.

My parents' lives drifted more and more apart. While my father spent most of his time in the business world, promoting and installing electronic data devices, my mother was mainly concerned about the environmental destruction and the injustice in the world. She travelled to South America, where her oldest sister lived, and told me later that if it hadn't been for us children, she would have stayed there to live and work with the poor. Often when my father was away for longer periods of time, one of her female friends would stay overnight and occupy his side of the bed. My father, too, did not always sleep on his own. He had various acquaintances in other places, one of whom was his secretary who he later moved in with.

When my father came home from his travels, he usually brought us gifts. He bought me many lovely soft toys, and the only book I have kept from my childhood is a Dutch version of Pipi Longstockings, as my father was working in Holland for many years. But at the same time, his home comings soon meant endless rows with my mother. Sometimes they argued about money, sometimes about politics, sometimes about her friends or the state of the house.

One night my father came home unexpectedly and found my mother in bed with her female friend. He was furious, calling her lesbian and throwing both of them out of the house. I don't know how my brother and sisters could sleep through the racket, but I woke up and witnessed the whole scene, crying and begging them to stop. When my mother and her friend had gone, my father brought me to bed, stroking my face (which I hated) and trying to explain that he had done the right thing.

It was soon clear that this couldn't go on for much longer, so they finally decided to separate and my father moved in with his secretary. However, he wouldn't simply leave us the house. After much to and fro with lawyers, when they officially divorced we had to give up the upper part of the house which was rented out to mature university students. I was 13 years old then, and to swap my bedroom for the former dining room was not easy. However, I kept the same furniture and arranged everything as it had been before. For my mother it was much harder, as she moved into the basement. My oldest sister left school that summer and went away to train on a farm. My other sister, who was developing a drug problem at that time, got the garden house, while my brother squeezed into my father's former study. In order to earn some money, my mother took in day-care-children, mainly babies whose parents went back to work.

There were other changes happening around us. The fields and woods we had played in so freely suddenly made room for a housing estate. A new school was built, the roads were tarred (they had been just sand before) and a bus service was introduced. The world of "Blue Bird" more and more disappeared. There were still places where Arthos and I could roam, but they became fewer and the danger of meeting other people increased. I was longing to get back to Ireland where my aunt had taken me and my brother on holidays the year before. There had been so much space. I began to save up my pocket money, so that one day I could buy a small farm in the west of Ireland. Often I would spend hours studying my school atlas to find the least populated places on earth. That's where I wanted to go, far away from the noise and the crowds and the misunderstandings.

It was not until I went to High School that I discovered the pleasure of reading stories. Information books, especially on history, geography and wildlife, had always interested me, but I seldom read fiction. When my school friend introduced me to her local library, I found whole shelves full of adventure books. The first ever book which captivated me so much that I couldn't put it down until it was finished, was the story of a boy in Iceland who rode off on his pony to look for some lost sheep and got trapped in a blizzard. Adventures like that were just the right fuel for my imagination. They had to be realistic (no fairies or goblins or talking animals), take place in nature and finish with a happy ending. Fantasies and Science Fiction didn't make sense to me, neither did the famous literature we had to study at school. Anything romantic simply bored me to death, and crime gave me nightmares and deepened my fear of people.

In those days we also got our first television at home, and although the high-pitched background noise (which human ears are not meant to pick up) gave me a headache, I loved watching adventure films, especially with a historical theme. After watching a film or reading a book, I went outside, dressed up appropriately to resemble the hero, and relived the story. So one day I would be swinging high in the apple tree with a long spy glass set in front of my eyes, being the sailor in the storm looking out for land. Another day I would tie an old blanket round a saw-horse and gallop across the fields with a war cry on my lips. It never occurred to me that there was anything odd about this, even at the age of 16 or 17. After all, the characters in the books and films had been real people and I was just like them.

Not only did I relive characters and adventures which had come to me through books and films, but I kept inventing my own, and after a while I began to write my stories down to share them with my friend at school. My very first story book, for which I was allowed to use my mother's typewriter, took place in Lapland. It had nothing to do with Santa Claus, though, whom I didn't believe in anyway, but was about a boy who went off to look for a stray reindeer. When he came back with it, his home lay in ashes, his parents were killed and their herd had been stolen. The boy chased the thieves and managed to bring his reindeers back, starting a new life on his own.

I have still got a box with about 30 stories written between the age of 13 and 17, each filling one or two school jotters and telling of children who fled from war, fought natural disasters or rescued animals. My friend at school was an encouraging fan of my stories, but none of my teachers ever took the time to read them. My brother often accused me of "talking like a book". Perhaps I spent so much time in my story world that I found it very hard to switch into every day communication. On the other hand, conversations had never come easily to me, because they didn't leave me enough time to carefully formulate what I wanted to say, which is the one aspect of writing that I have always valued most.

My parents' marriage break-up affected each member of our family. As mentioned earlier, my second sister, then 15 years old, developed a drug problem. She was dyslexic and couldn't keep up at school which, especially for my father, was seen as a failure. It also later came to light that he had sexually abused her. So in order to escape the pain and the problems at home and at school, she began to smoke cannabis, then took LSD and eventually injected heroin. My mother, who was struggling with her own life, tried to help her as best as she could, but there was more needed to break an addiction like that than motherly concern. One of the students from upstairs had long conversations with my sister, trying to persuade her to accept professional help. Their voices and the cigarette smoke kept me awake at night, until I decided to sleep in the old stable where my oldest sister's pony had lived. But many a night I had to flee from there, too, when my sister and her friends played loud music in the garden house. Once I was so angry for being kept awake, that I took the axe and began to split wood. My mother was furious with me for making such a noise in the middle of the night. I couldn't see the difference between my sister's racket and the dull blows of the axe. However, from then on I would take Arthos and my blanket and go in search of a quiet hiding place in the woods.

It was my brother's eleventh birthday. He had some friends round for games and cake. When they had left, my mother took the two of us aside and asked: "Don't you miss someone?" We were both thinking hard. Had my brother forgotten to invite somebody? Perhaps my mother's younger sister should have been there? We didn't know the answer. Then my mother told us quite matter of fact that my sister had been rushed to hospital after a suicide attempt in the school's toilets. I swallowed once or twice and didn't say anything, neither did my brother. To be honest, part of me was relieved that my sister was somewhere else. I had suffered enough from her, not just the disturbed nights and the teasing and taunting. But surely I didn't want her to die. I just wanted her to change, to be nicer.

Two teachers at school made my life a misery at that time. One of them was our Latin teacher. She was an elderly lady who had probably never heard about psychology and forgotten what it felt like to be a child. Perhaps she even had a streak of sadism in her, but it might have been unintentional. In any case, her manner scared me so much that when asked to respond to her questions or to translate a passage of *De Bello Gallico* in front of the class, I couldn't utter a word. Vocabulary or grammar which I had happily recited to my friend a minute before the teacher entered the room suddenly vanished from my mind. The worst was that she constantly accused me of being lazy and not doing my homework which infuriated me, as I would never leave a duty undone and Latin used to be one of my favourite subjects in the past.

On the eve before my sister was due to come home from hospital, I knelt at my window sill and for the first time folded my hands to pray. "God, if you can hear me and if you care enough, please let my sister be kind when she comes home tomorrow and please let the Latin teacher be off", I said, wondering what would happen. This teacher had never been off. Her immune system must have been as hard and impenetrable as her manners. However, the next day at school we were told that we could go home an hour earlier, as Latin was cancelled. Coming home, I found my sister in the kitchen, stirring a spaghetti sauce. "I made you something else, since you don't like spicy stuff", she greeted me. I was so surprised that I could hardly believe my ears. After dinner I went straight to my bedroom and knelt by the window again. "My God, you've done it. You've heard me. You're really there…"

For the rest of the day I floated half-way between heaven and earth. I was overwhelmed by the experience that God had answered my prayers. At the same time I started to tremble. If God knew me so well, he also knew my dark side, the rage, the greed and all the stuff that I wish was not part of me. Yes, it was great to know God so close at my side, to be able to share everything with him as I had done in the past with my angel Cari. But surely, there was also an obligation on my part to become a better person. I raked through my brain to make a list of all that I knew about God. There wasn't very much. I knew the Ten Commandments and the Lord's Prayer. I also had a vessel for Holy Water which I had brought back from Ireland. So I hung this vessel up above my bed in the stable and filled it with water. I dedicated a little cushion which I had once knitted to be a prayer cushion and placed it in front of the vessel. Every morning and every night I would kneel down, kiss the cushion three times before placing my folded hands on it and say the Lord's Prayer. After adding my personal prayers, I would wet my forefinger in the Holy Water and make the sign of the cross on my forehead before getting up. It became a ritual which I adhered to for several years.

Chapter 5: Losing Control

When I was ten years old, we went on a family holiday to Corsica where, because of the heat, I suddenly fainted. From then on I turned my back on hot countries, and when my relatives invited me to visit them in South America, I declined. But I fainted again, and this time it had more far reaching consequences than the first time.

I was singing in the school choir, and being one of the smallest in the first soprano, I had to stand in the front row on the stage. We were supposed to dress up in black and white. As I didn't have black shoes, I cleaned my black wellies and put my trousers over them to hide the shaft. With the spotlights right on me and the audience filling every space in the hall, I soon grew hot. We were in the middle of a dramatic part of the Christmas Oratorium, when the music in front of my eyes became blurred. Within a few seconds my eyesight was gone, then my hearing vanished and I collapsed straight into the arms of the conductor. He had no choice but to carry me off the stage. When my senses returned, I found myself in a small room with some teachers and students fussing over me. They helped me onto a chair and offered me a glass of water which I took with trembling hands, spilling half of it over my blouse. I felt close to panic, especially when the well meaning people stroked my shoulder and tried to hold my hand. "Don't touch me, please!" I wanted to scream, but I could hardly breathe, let alone speak.

The incident was so traumatic for me that I left the choir. Concerts with the orchestra were slightly easier, since I always had a seat, playing the cello. Even so, the fear of fainting sometimes overcame me so strongly that I nearly fainted from fear. In class I soon lost the confidence to go up to the blackboard when asked to demonstrate a sum or to explain a figure. It even became so bad that I couldn't enter a shop or visit the dentist for fear of passing out, and finally I could no longer use the train. I think what I really feared was to lose control, to be at the mercy of people who handled me, touched me or moved me somewhere without my knowing. I had always had a tendency to claustrophobia, a fear of being stuck, imprisoned, unable to escape. I never locked toilet doors, for example, too scared that they wouldn't open again. At school, my friend always stood guard for me. In other places I simply took the risk of being embarrassed.

Another problem which I developed during those days was the fear of shouting out obscene words or phrases. Sometimes I was so scared of it that I put my hand over my mouth to make sure that no word escaped my lips. Much later I found out that these were the symptoms of Tourette's syndrome. I rarely took part in lessons now and my written work suffered, too, as I needed all my energy to keep my mind under control.

Travelling to and from school became more and more of a struggle. Apart from the fears of fainting, I was scared to suddenly open the door between two stations (which in those days was possible) and to jump out. I didn't want to kill myself, but something inside me tried to force me to. My school friend was the only person I told about this, and only after she promised to keep it a secret. Sometimes I walked all the way to her station, which took me about an hour, to enter the train with her. I urged her to hold me back if ever she saw me making for the doors while the train was in motion. She often accompanied me to my station in the afternoon and then travelled back. Without her support I would not have managed to go to school at all.

Nevertheless, there came a time when the stress became too much for me and instead of going to school, I hid in the forest. It took almost two weeks, before my mother found out about it. She was very angry, accusing me of deliberately causing trouble when she had more than enough on her plate. I didn't know how to explain what was going on inside me. I mentioned the fear of fainting, so she took me to see our GP about that. He thought it was a growth problem, since I was quite skinny, and prescribed medication to aid my circulation. I was too scared of being locked up in a psychiatric hospital as to disclose the full picture of what was troubling me.

My second sister left home not long after her 16th birthday. She had been offered a place in a Rehabilitation Centre for drug addicts. However, she must have passed her stereo recorder and rock music tapes on to my brother, because soon I could hear the same noise coming from his room.

Right from birth I had been extremely sensitive to sound. Certain sounds seem to pierce straight through my skin, causing me physical pain as well as general stress. Loud noises like food mixers, Hoovers, washing machines, strimmers, motorbikes, pneumatic hammers and jets are so painful that I need to cover my ears. The sounds of rock music must have got exactly the same qualities. I simply can't bear it. It hurts too much. So as soon as my brother put his tapes on, I had to flee. Fortunately, my mother was never keen on this type of music and had more control over my brother than she had had over my sister. But I was often called intolerant for not being able to put up with it even for a short time, as if you were accusing someone of intolerance who is allergic to dairy products or can't go near a hayfield.

While my mother and brother spent the summer holidays with our relatives in South America, I joined my aunt horse trekking in the west of Ireland. Meanwhile I was learning English at school, but it caused me a lot of difficulty. Unlike Latin, German and Dutch, which was pronounced the same way it was written, the sounds of English words hardly ever resembled the letters used for them. It was a confusing language with seemingly no structure at all, and yet it was so important to me to master it, since I still held on to my dream of living on a small farm in Ireland. I might have picked up a lot by listening to other people's conversations, but I'm afraid I didn't have much patience for that. I preferred to escape to the hills and the cliffs, away from people whose presence meant having to constantly keep a grip on those fears and compulsive thoughts which threatened to break out at any moment.

When we came back from Ireland, my aunt had to go away for a few days. She asked me whether I wanted to visit my grandparents or stay in her flat on my own. I thought it would be quite nice to have the place to myself, although I didn't know anyone in her town who I could turn to in an emergency. My aunt probably didn't think of that or she might not have left me, not quite 15 years of age, on my own. During the day, it wasn't too bad. I went on long bicycle tours and had picnics in the forest, cooling my feet in a wayside burn and enjoying the music of the birds. But as soon as I entered the flat, I was overwhelmed by fear.

My main fear in those days was of killing myself. I have to stress that I didn't want to do it. I desperately wanted to live. But just as shouting out obscene words was absolutely against my will and the more I fought it, the stronger the fear of doing it, so it was with suicide. I prayed. I tried to distract myself with reading or watching the telly. I wrote down that I wanted to live. Yet all the time, the urge to cut my veins or to strangle myself with the wire of the ceiling light or to stick my fingers in one of the electric sockets grew stronger. Finally, I threw all the sharp kitchen knives behind the living room unit where my hands couldn't reach them. I pushed heavy furniture against the wall sockets and avoided looking at the ceiling lights. I don't know how I managed to get the flat back to normal the day my aunt came back, but as far as I know, she never found out how much I had suffered in her absence.

Ever since God had answered my first prayers (and he answered many more), I was keen to go to church. Our village church was virtually dead. Once when I went to the morning service, the bell ringer asked me: "What do you want here?" He couldn't understand that I was seeking to know more about God. Young people weren't supposed to be interested in religion. So I sat amongst half a dozen elderly ladies, not understanding much of the old hymns or the minister's sermon. It was my Latvian grandmother who proposed to me to attend confirmation classes, and my mother found a church a little further away whose minister was happy for me to join a group of young people under his instruction. It was a very important experience for me. In October (I was 15 years old then) we stayed in a simple mountain hut for a week, studying, apart from the Bible, the Diary of Anne Frank. One day we had a very wet excursion, getting lost in the forest and coming back soaked to the skin, when I discovered that for the first time I had my period. I was rather unprepared and too embarrassed to ask one of the other girls to help me out with towels. Somehow I had always assumed that I would never become a woman. In fact, I was still Blue Bird, the Red Indian boy, or Einar from Iceland, who rescued the lost sheep, or one of my own invented heroes, always boys, always about 12 years old, always loners. I didn't want to grow up.

The following winter, my grandmother in Frankfurt died. It happened quite suddenly and she died at home in her own bed, cared for by her oldest daughter, who had arrived from South America as soon as she heard the diagnosis. My granny had a brain tumour, too advanced for surgery. She was given six weeks to live, which was exactly what she had. One day my mother picked me up from school and brought me to the airport. I wanted to protest, being scared of planes and not having had time to get used to the thought and prepare myself, but I had no choice. My granny was dying and she wanted to say good bye to me.
In fact, when I arrived she was already so confused that I wasn't sure whether she recognised me. She sent me to buy a special cake which I had never heard of. When I came back with the cake, she was asleep.
My grandfather took her death very badly. He thought he couldn't live without her and began to drink to cope with his grief. I loved my granny dearly, but I was happy for her to go to heaven. I never had a doubt that God would welcome her with open arms, even though she hadn't been a member of a church. Many years later, my aunt, who had cared for her up to her death, told me that my granny had seen a bright light at the end of a tunnel, which she longed for, but couldn't reach. My aunt suggested to her that the light was God himself and what she needed to meet him was forgiveness through Jesus. So my granny asked for a minister, one of my father's relatives, who came

immediately and prayed with her. After that she died in peace.

Since my fear of losing control grew worse and my grades suffered badly, I couldn't see myself staying on at school. First, my mother didn't want to know about me leaving after year 10. "You're too young! You're too gifted! Just pull yourself together!" was her answer. She didn't understand that the more I pulled myself together, the worse it all became. Finally she realised that she couldn't persuade me to stay on, so she insisted that I became an apprentice like my oldest sister and helped me find such a place.
I had always felt more relaxed in nature than in built-up places. In fact, I had often watched the shepherd going past at the other side of the wall with his flock, his dogs and his donkey cart. I had studied books about sheep rearing and written a long essay about it for school. I could imagine myself walking from place to place with a flock of sheep and at night sitting by the campfire, cuddling my dogs. However, this was probably a very romantic notion of a shepherd's life. In reality you had to be strong and tough, preferably a boy, and I was skinny and immature. Since farmers didn't want to take me on either, I was finally grateful for an apprenticeship in gardening. In order to obtain my leaving certificate from school, I had to persuade the chemistry, biology and physics teacher to give me a pass mark. Only the Latin teacher was immovable, but I could make up for it with my high grade in music.

Chapter 6: The Nightmare continues

In the summer after I left school, I was invited to join some of my cousins on a walking tour from youth hostel to youth hostel. Since we lived so far apart, we hadn't seen much of each other during our childhood. We were all descendents of my father's mother who had been forced to flee from Latvia when the Communists took over. I soon discovered that with some of them I had quite a lot in common. First, each of us lacked the usual art of socialising and we related to one another more through what we did than through words. Secondly, we all spoke a rather formal High German and had not really developed any local accent. And thirdly, we shared very similar interests, like hill walking, classical music, a Christian faith and a concern for nature. We also found common ground in our highly academic thinking. In fact, several of my cousins later won scholarships to universities, having achieved the best A-levels of their year group. At the same time we were all clad in second-hand or home-made clothes, the boys cut each other's hair, while the girls let theirs grow, and we would rather deprive ourselves of ice cream than miss a visit to the local museum. I felt a kinship with them which I hadn't experienced before.

At the end of the summer I started my apprenticeship. I had anticipated it with mixed feelings, but I wasn't prepared for what was to come. Every morning I had to get up at 5 o'clock and cycle eight miles to work. This didn't matter too much to me, since I had always been an early riser. The work itself, loading wheelbarrows with compost or digging earth and planting trees, was also bearable, although painful for my body and boring for my mind. What I found hardest to come to terms with were my colleagues. In a way, I was right back at the village school, only six years further on. All that the people seemed to be interested in was money, drink and sex, perhaps fashion (the women) and football (the men).

I didn't suffer so much from my fears of fainting, of shouting obscene words or the compulsion to commit suicide, but instead I began to suffer from the monotony of the tasks and from lack of intellectual stimulation. Sometimes I set myself maths challenges to solve in my head or I recited Latin grammar. At other times I made up stories or held discussions with politicians about environmental issues or international affairs. And sometimes, when there was nothing to distract myself with, I would hear the plants or the tools talk to me. I didn't hear them with my ears. I rather perceived their message without sounds or gestures. I knew what they were thinking and feeling and what they wanted to communicate to me. They were like the little elephant that my brother had rejected and which I had rescued out of compassion. Sometimes they just smiled at me or thanked me for watering and feeding them. At other times they could be quite demanding. "You gave the other tree more compost than me. Come back, I'm still hungry!" or:

"I want you to clean my blade first, before you clean the rake. I worked much harder, digging all this ground!" Some of the larger trees wanted me to pat them and greet them. If I forgot, they would cry in despair. If I remembered, they were happy, but soon other trees asked for the same treatment, until I could hardly keep up with their demands. Part of me knew, of course, that plants and tools and other objects couldn't possibly have thoughts and feelings like that, but at the same time their cries were so clear that ignoring them felt impossible. Perhaps I can compare it to a 5-year old giving a tea party to her dolls and teddies. If one is missed out, she will surely hear it cry. How do you grow out of this? Perhaps it's just one area in which my mind stopped developing.

Shortly after I had started my apprenticeship, I celebrated my confirmation. It was a special occasion for me to affirm my faith in front of the congregation and to receive the minister's blessing. Of course, it was slightly spoilt by my fear of saying the wrong things or of fainting, but I always look back on it as an important milestone in my life. My Latvian grandmother and my godmother, who had been a missionary in Africa, gave me some treasured books which helped me to grow in my faith and in understanding the Bible. In fact, the assurance that my life was safe in God's hand, whatever happened to me, enabled me to face many situations which otherwise I would have turned away from.

That same year we moved again. My mother had been looking everywhere for a smaller house, since my father wanted to sell the one we had built. She finally found a semidetached garden house with 2 ½ rooms the other side of Rudow, almost next to the Berlin wall, which she could afford to buy. I never liked it, yet it was still better than a city flat. Arthos didn't like it either. One day, when we had all gone out, he managed to open the garden gate and ran all the way back to our old house. Well, just like me, he had to get used to the change. My mother got the biggest room, which also served as the living room. The other full-sized room was for me, but in addition to my bed it had a bunk bed for my sisters or other visitors and it also housed my brother's wardrobe, since he had to make do with the little box-room behind the kitchen. In a way, I had no real privacy anymore, no space in which to maintain my order. My oldest sister was visiting quite frequently and usually brought a friend along. I often escaped their conversations to sleep on Arthos' mattress, where I found more peace and quiet.

In winter, when thick snow covered the ground and the trees, I was required to work in the greenhouses. I remember planting thousands of tiny geraniums, row after row after row. The task itself, although dull and boring, would have been bearable, if it hadn't been for the radio blaring in the background. The noise prevented me from following my usual mathematical or political excursions and drove me to the edge of madness. So I was always the first one to volunteer to bring more compost in or to carry empty boxes away, just to get a few minutes of silence now and again.

One day a week I was attending the College of Agriculture to learn the theory behind the practice. It was a welcome change to the workplace. The botanical names of plants were easy for me to learn, since I understood the Latin meaning of them. Maths was my favourite subject and everything else was easy enough as well. We were never asked to come to the blackboard and we rarely had class discussions. It was rather a matter of listening to lectures, taking notes and asking questions if anything needed to be clarified. I could cope with that. My lunch I usually ate outside in the park or, if it was too cold and wet, in one of the greenhouses in the college grounds. In the beginning I was sometimes joined by another girl, until she left to emigrate to Canada.

One winter, I knitted myself over-trousers out of different coloured wool. They fitted perfectly and protected me from the snow. I was used to being laughed at for my clothes, but when I wore these trousers to college, I didn't just meet the usual taunting and sneering, but outright anger. I still don't understand what made these young boys and girls so angry. Was it simply because I dared to be different? What harm could multi-coloured knitted over-trousers possibly do to anyone? And yet, they hurled their insults at me, threatened to rip my trousers off me and finally even spat at my leather satchel which contained my books and folders. I tried my best to ignore them, all the time wondering what was going on in their minds. The spittle upset me most. It was bad enough to be touched by someone, but to find part of their insides on my property almost made me sick. I wiped the satchel with grass and later thoroughly washed it.

The following summer, my "Ireland"-aunt took me and my cousin Hilde on a hiking tour to Norway. There I had my first high mountain experience which almost cost me my life. With my hopeless sense of orientation, I climbed the Gaustatoppen from its steepest side, losing my aunt and my cousin and getting stuck on a vertical wall. I knew instinctively that I mustn't give in to fear. If I began to tremble, I was gone. So I prayed instead and hummed a simple tune, whilst rocking slightly from side to side, which had always been a good way to calm myself. After a while I noticed a ledge which I hadn't seen before. If I stretched out my arm, I could just reach it. So I went on, upwards, still humming the tune, still praying, until I reached the edge of the cliff and emerged at a boulder field leading to the top of the mountain. My cousin somehow managed to get up on a different route. My aunt, having more sense, preferred to walk around to the other side and called the Rescue out for us.
This wasn't our only adventure on the tour. A few nights later, while we were camping in front of a wooden cabin – the only dry and even spot to pitch a tent -, we were suddenly woken by a masked man who pointed a shotgun at us. It took my aunt several

hours of negotiation, while I was trembling and praying in the tent, before he finally let us go. My love for high mountains was kindled, while my fear of people had grown.

My second year as a gardener apprentice was in some ways worse than the first one. I simply had enough of the job and the place. I also felt terribly lonely. My mother was very concerned about the fact that I had no friends and spent all my spare time locked in my own world or roaming the fields and woods with Arthos. She was so desperate to see me mixing with other young people that once, while we were doing the dishes together, she shouted at me: "Other girls at your age have boy friends. Marietta (my sister's friend) even has a baby, and you have no friends at all! You have to make an effort!" Her words just hurt and showed me how little she understood. Yes, I was desperate for people I could relate to, people like my cousins, but such folks seemed to be so rare. When I left school, I also left the orchestra, and the chances of finding likeminded people amongst my fellow gardeners were nil. Mixing with people whose world I didn't understand, nor share, only left me exhausted and empty.

When the trees lost their leaves and the autumn mists crawled in, I longed to die. What was the point of carrying on? All this effort to keep my fears under control. All these slow moving days of excruciating boredom. All the misunderstanding, the teasing and taunting. I had enough of it. I couldn't take anymore.

I had no energy left to pull myself together, to keep going in hope of a better future. I looked at Arthos, my faithful friend, the one I loved most in the world. I felt guilty when I thought of abandoning him, but that grey autumn day even he couldn't hold me back. I climbed to the top of the highest tree I could find in the forest and threw myself head-first down.

Well, God must have despatched a dozen angels to protect me, for by the time I landed at the bottom, my fall had been slowed by so many branches that I was virtually unhurt. My first reaction was not relief, though, but anger. "Can I not even kill myself?" I shouted. Then I grabbed a branch, which had come down with me, and hit my left hand with it until it began to swell. I looked at it for a while, not feeling the pain. Finally I decided to go home. I told my mother that I had fallen out of a tree and showed her my swollen hand. She took me to the doctor, but urged me not to mention the tree. "Just say that you fell. At your age people don't climb trees anymore." Whatever the doctor made of it, for the next two weeks I didn't have to go to work and after that I somehow managed to keep going.

It was the same hand that began to give me more and more trouble. First it was just painful. Then I would occasionally lose my grip on things. Once I broke a whole pack of twenty flowerpots which simply crashed to the ground. Then, one day, a strange looking hump appeared on the upper side of my wrist. It grew and made my hand stiffer and stiffer. So my mother finally sent me to the doctor. He took one look and sent me straight to hospital for a wrist operation.

I didn't like the crowded hospital dorm, although I was fortunate not to be laid in the corridor. I read my little prayer book, which my godmother had sent me, and was convinced that after the operation I would wake up in heaven. So when I found myself back in the hospital dorm, I was quite disappointed. My wrist was too tightly bandaged and I suffered enormous pain the night after the operation. However, I thought this was normal, part of being in hospital, and so I didn't ring for the nurse. When she came in the next morning, she was aghast and so was the doctor. My hand had swollen so much, that it took six weeks and many doses of antibiotics to save it. By then, my apprenticeship was almost over. I had some written and practical exams, which I passed without problems, and was finally free to leave for Ireland.

My colleagues at work had bought a present for me and expected me to come and receive it. However, I couldn't face going to the place again, and when the boss phoned up and offered to bring the present round, I said I was already packed for Ireland and didn't have time. Later I often felt ashamed about my reaction, but at the time I just couldn't face the prospect of meeting any of these people again. I hope they were able to forgive me.

Chapter 7: Dogs and Children

When I left home, I knew that I left for good. My brother was desperate to get out of the box-room, and it was no question that he moved into my room as soon as I was gone. Most of my childhood treasures were packed away in the attic, especially my large collection of soft toys which I later donated to a home for teenage mothers whose babies were overjoyed at the arrival of my animals, so I was told. One cuddly dog, though, I never gave away and over the years he has travelled everywhere with me: Matty or Matthew Maguire, named after my classmate Matthew who bought him for me for my eleventh birthday.

Saying good bye to Arthos was probably the hardest step. From now on, my brother would care for him. One of my mother's friends had put me in contact with people who ran an organic farm in County Leitrim and let me live with them for a while. For the next six years this became my refuge, although I could only stay there for a few months at a time. When I arrived, I pitched my little tent behind the house and made friends with Rataplan, the dog, who followed me everywhere. Barbara, an early retired social worker, had bought the tumble-down farmstead for her son who renovated and cultivated it bit by bit with the help of his mother and people like myself who came and went over the years.
My first task was to dig terraces into the steep hillside for planting vegetables. It was hard work, but

meanwhile my body had grown strong. Whenever I stopped to take a rest, my eyes would gaze over the hills and lochs around me which gave me a sense of freedom and belonging. I suffered much less from my fears and compulsive rituals than before. It might partly have been due to the people I lived with, who were all in a sense "odd balls" like me. My clothes, my speech and my mannerisms, like rocking or hand flapping which, when necessary, I had learned to suppress, were simply accepted, and so was the fact that I didn't like to be touched, often withdrew into my own world and had a rather limited diet. But I still felt very lonely, even more so when I saw the others relate to each other in such a hearty way and I didn't know how to be part of it.

In my free time I explored the mountains at the back with Rataplan close at my heels. I climbed vertical cliffs with my bare toes and fingertips holding on to the tiniest cracks. I swam in rock pools to cool down and sheltered in caves from rain and thunderstorms. Once I fell into a bog hole and would have drowned if Rataplan hadn't pulled me out. From then on I carefully watched the colour of the vegetation and soon learned where it was safe to put my feet. Up there I was a 12-year old boy again, no longer Blue Bird, the Red Indian, but Merrill, an Irish orphan who lived wild in the hills. He later became the main character in "The Silent Cry", the first of my novels to be published.

Although I felt sad to leave Ireland, I knew that I couldn't stay on the farm indefinitely. It soon became too cold in my tent and there wasn't enough room in the still unfinished farmhouse. I was also feeling restless, still haunted by the question what life was all about. So I went back to Germany, not to my mother, but to my cousins to whom I felt a deeper kinship. My uncle found me a job on a nearby farm, where I instantly befriended the St. Bernhard dog and a shy little boy, but otherwise didn't like it very much.

One of my cousins got married and with her gardener husband wanted to revive a big orchard, which had been handed down in the family. They invited me to live and work with them. I remember every morning writing up a list of tasks needing to be done, which I later ticked off as I worked my way through them. My cousin's husband soon realised that giving me too many tasks at once would put me under a lot of pressure, as I didn't know where to start and somehow felt that I had to finish everything before I could take a break.

Again, much of the work was back breaking and I did actually damage my lower back which has caused me chronic pain over the years. But I also had the satisfaction of planning and calculating, especially for the large vegetable plot which was my sole responsibility. My cousin soon gave birth to a little boy, Jonathan, who together with the dogs gave me much joy. In fact, it was Jonathan who helped me most to overcome my fear of human touch. He was forever out in the garden with me. I even took him up the fruit trees to the horror of his mother, and he was barely a year old when he knew how to pick red currants. I think it was the clumsiness and innocence of his movements that made me accept and even enjoy his touch. Like the dogs, he showed his affection naturally, without expecting anything in return.

During the busy summer months, some of my other cousins came to help. I remember one of them, who had just started on a degree in mathematics, suddenly shouting out with excitement: "I've got it! I've found a new formula for solving..." Whatever it was, he embarked on a long lecture about this particular mathematical problem, completely oblivious that none of us was able to follow him. However, it fascinated me, not the mathematical formula, but the fact that it was so important for him to share it with us. I had long given up trying to share my fascinations with others, as my parents and siblings had made it too clear that it got on their nerves.

With Hilde and Martin, my closest cousins, I would go on long walks and bicycle tours, exploring historic places or watching rare animals. Once we had been working very hard all day in the dusty heat and decided to go to the church hall, where we were allowed to use the piano, to play some music together. After washing off the day's sweat, Martin decided to put his pyjamas on. Thus he was ready to cycle to church. Even I knew that it was a bit odd to go out in pyjamas, but he couldn't see the point. They were fresh and clean – why should anyone object?

Being with my cousins and observing them gave me some insight into my own "oddities" and into other people's reactions to them.

Jonathan's parents were members of the local Baptist Church and I was soon baptised there, too, more to please them than out of conviction, since I was baptised and confirmed already. On the morning of my baptism I had a vision while I was praying. I was looking into a deep dark hole, when suddenly out of nowhere a huge stone was rolled over it to seal it up. Without being told, I knew that it was a symbol for God sealing the "black hole" of fears and compulsive thoughts which haunted me so much at day and night. A great relief swept through me and yet, at the same time I somehow knew that one day the hole had to open again to let me face and come to terms with what lay at the bottom.

During the following years I became very involved at church, which made up for the monotony I often felt in my job. I joined the youth choir, which every Sunday afternoon went out to sing in the nursing home, the hospital, the prison or the pedestrian zone. I freely "gave testimony" how Jesus had saved me and changed my life and I even made an effort to look at people, although I have always found eye contact very distracting. One day I was approached about helping with the weekly children's club in a nearby town. Most of the children came from broken homes and had rather sad lives. They soaked up the Bible stories I was telling them with my little felt puppets and the message that Jesus cared about them and wanted to be their friend. As with Jonathan and the dogs, I would tumble around with these kids, not feeling in the least threatened by their touch, and I gradually learned to handle gentler affection as well.

I still suffered from depression and loneliness, but less than before. I also suffered from homesickness for Ireland, and whenever there was a quiet period in the garden, I travelled across to the Leitrim Mountains. Once my oldest sister and I cycled down the whole west coast of Ireland, staying and working on organic farms. While for my sister it was just an extended holiday, I was desperately searching for a place to settle down. By that time my dream had changed from having my own little farm to living in a Community of like-minded people. In fact, this idea grew steadily in my mind, until some 12 years later I wrote it down in detail in a booklet I called "The Celtic Christian Community – a vision". I even had my eyes on a small island in the Outer Hebrides with a deserted village on it, which was for sale at the time. However, my dream never materialised, and so at the end of three months I returned to my cousin in Germany, whereas my sister went to South America, where she has lived ever since, to work with the poor and downtrodden.

Around my 20th birthday, my cousin Martin and I went on a wilderness tour in Lapland. Hilde was meant to join us, but she took ill just before we were due to leave. It certainly was a wilderness experience, as we walked off the map and got lost for several days, running out of food and almost drowned whilst crossing a fast flowing stream. However, one of the outcomes of the tour was that Martin developed feelings of affection for me which I found rather confusing. I wasn't ready for a lover. I was just learning to enjoy the physical affections of children, but most people of my own age I still kept at bay. I asked his sister to explain this to him and felt sorry and somewhat guilty for upsetting him. In the end it was agreed that Martin would stop visiting us for a while until his feelings for me had cooled down. During one of the last times we met, I was trying to explain to him my reasons for leaving school, that it hadn't been lack of academic interest or ability, but my fears of fainting or jumping off the train. He suddenly looked at me and said that he knew what I was talking about, as he felt the same, especially on undergrounds. I wasn't sure what to make of this. Part of me thought that he just wanted to show sympathy for me, but I was soon to learn otherwise.

My life at church and with my cousin's family carried on much as before. One day a Glaswegian-American family moved into the area and started a small House Church, reaching out especially to British soldiers and their families who were stationed there. I joined their Bible study group, mainly to practise my English, and later became good friends with them.

A year after our wilderness tour something happened that rolled away the stone from the dark hole and shattered my life: Martin's body was found in pieces on the underground line in Berlin. His twin brother was called to confirm identification. At his funeral I wept in sorrow and confusion. "Why did God let it happen?" was the most urgent question on my mind.

"And if it happened to Martin, could it also happen to me?" All the old suicidal fears were suddenly back with a force I had never felt before. The compulsion to kill myself was so strong that I fled to Ireland to seek refuge in the mountains, but even there the cliffs beckoned me to throw myself down into the abyss. There was no escape. I remember once changing trains in Hastings after a short spell in a Christian Community in Kent. The urge to jump in front of the arriving train was so strong that I desperately clung to the pillar in the middle of the platform, begging God to hold me back.

When I was back with my cousin, she made contact with a Christian counselling centre, where a kind woman regularly gave us some help and advice. The House Church couple, Brian and Linda, invited me to start a Sunday school and asked me to give cello lessons to one of their very musical sons. Linda was one of the first adults who I voluntarily embraced, and in her arms I always felt safe. I carried on writing stories, sometimes simple parables for the kids at the children's club or at Sunday school, but also longer ones, usually about children who were misunderstood and fled from a world in which they didn't fit in.
Through the Baptist Youth Movement I met a young pastor who pointed me to a number of books which explained my obsessive-compulsive thoughts and behaviour, and in his counselling sessions I was able to confront some of my fears.
About two years after Martin's death, I used my savings and the quiet winter months to attend a

Christian Language school in Yorkshire. Several people at church had pointed out that I had a gift for working with children, especially the ones that other adults found so hard to understand. Was God calling me into the Children's Ministry? The possibility of going to Bible College had been on my mind for some time. Once I had a vision of a Celtic woman coming towards me over green hills with the words: "We need you, too!" I had always taken it for a call to Ireland, though the time had obviously not been ripe yet. However, the ten weeks in Whitby would hopefully help me to perfect my grammar, spelling and pronunciation of the English language and lead on to Bible College or whatever else was to open up.

I very much enjoyed my time at the language school in the company of Christians from all over the world. I loved studying as much as exploring the wild winter coast and the Yorkshire moors, and I enjoyed singing together and passing exams with distinction. But at the same time I was always aware of my inability to socialise and make friends like other people and still used up a lot of my energy to suppress fears, battle with compulsive thoughts and carry out rituals demanded by objects around me. However, when I returned to Germany at the end of March, I knew that it would only be for one more summer before I was to embark on a 3-years course at Northumbria Bible College. At last, the future looked brighter. The boredom of digging and weeding and harvesting would soon be over. Little did I know that my plans were not to work out.

Chapter 8: In Hospital

Jonathan was by now almost 5 years old and had a little sister, Annie, who was beginning to walk. In the evenings we often went out on our bicycles with Annie in the child seat and the dogs running happily along. This would give my cousin and her husband some time to themselves. They also held times of family worship in a little chapel in the basement of their house.

However, for me these times were far from happy. I hadn't noticed it so much before I went to Whitby, but having experienced joyful positive worship there, the times in the basement chapel felt very depressing and I began to dread them. Several times I went hiding in the orchard until the time of morning or evening worship had passed. I think, my cousin was just sad that I didn't want to attend, but her husband felt that I was a bad example for the children who might soon want to stay away, too. I tried to do them the favour of being present, but the turmoil it created in me was not worth it. The kind of God, my cousin's husband wanted me to worship, was like a policeman, ready to punish us for every evil thought which came to our mind. The dilemma for me was that my mind was full of evil thoughts (especially suicidal ones) which I had absolutely no control over. If they deserved punishment, I should have been punished all day. My cousin's husband was puzzled by this and the only explanation he could come up with was that I had evil spirits living in me. During the next few weeks he fervently prayed over me to drive them out, and when no change occurred, he accused me of holding back some secret sin. All this became too much for me. I was suffering enough from the malfunctions of my mind. Having to search for secret sins on top of it brought me to the edge of sanity. I could no longer pray freely, which had been my most effective "weapon" in the daily battle with my compulsions and fears. I knew I was breaking down unless I broke out, and so one day I stole away on the train, not quite sure where to go. I ended up at the Counselling Centre, but the lady who had supported us over the years was not there. Instead, the director himself had a long talk with me and also phoned my cousin. I stayed overnight and was called for another talk the next morning, in which he persuaded me to see a psychiatrist. He gave me the name and address of one near where I lived and assured me that it was safe to return to my cousin.

We agreed that I didn't have to take part in family worship and that my cousin's husband would leave me alone with his "evil-spirit-theory". In turn, I had to make an appointment with the psychiatrist, who happened to be on holiday for a few weeks, and promised my cousin to let her know when I felt I couldn't cope anymore.
In my spare time I was working on another manuscript, Merrill's story, which was later called "The Silent Cry". The inspiration came partly from a book called "Robbie", which I had found on Linda's

bookshelf and instantly devoured. Robbie was an autistic child who was befriended by a care-worker. To me it was an eye-opener, as I found so many of my own traits in the boy that I sometimes felt as though I was looking into a mirror. Although I hadn't come across any formal studies of Autism then, the character of Merrill in "The Silent Cry" was by later critics often called autistic. I simply clothed some of my own feelings and experiences with the Irish orphan on the Slieve Anierin Mountain, as I had done so often while I was there. The novel simply poured out of me, mainly during the night, and the handwritten manuscript was finished within six weeks. The editing and typing, besides my gardening work, took me about three months.

The summer was drawing to an end, when I finally got an appointment with the psychiatrist. He sent me a questionnaire to fill in beforehand and to bring along. I was understandably nervous when I entered his room and took a seat next to his big desk, but no more nervous than at seeing a doctor for one of my many injuries, like falling off a ladder or stepping into a garden fork. However, he took one look at me and skimmed through the questionnaire, before he slowly nodded and said: "I think, I'll have to send you to hospital." This came as a complete shock to me. I hadn't battled on all my life just to be locked up when things finally promised to improve. Another month and I was going to start Bible College. Couldn't he offer me a few sessions or a few tips to make those fears and compulsions go away? He said he couldn't.

A few sessions were not enough, and someone as suicidal as I needed to be looked after full time. I swallowed. Perhaps I had made a mistake on the questionnaire or he had misunderstood some of my answers. I tried to explain that I was really coping quite well, but he threw in some questions and remarks which caught me off-guard and only confirmed his opinion. In the end, he lent me a book of essays written by staff and patients of a Christian Psychiatric Clinic north of Frankfurt, which he had in mind for me. Then he gave me an appointment a fortnight later and let me go.

Cycling home, I was nearly knocked over by a car, as I was too confused to pay proper attention to the traffic. All I could think of was: "I'm not going to hospital, never! I'm going to Bible College and I don't care what anyone else says! I'm going to show you that I can make it! Nobody's going to lock me up, ever!"

The book was very interesting. Psychiatric hospitals had certainly changed from the padded cells, electro shocks and straight jackets I had heard of during my childhood. I also learned that there were many other people who, like me, suffered from fears and compulsions which they couldn't control. Perhaps it wasn't such a bad idea to give it a try. However, I was all set for Bible College. I had even bought a skirt, although I had never worn one before. When I went back to the psychiatrist, I was still pretty sure that I was not going along with his plans. I don't know how he did it, but I suppose, being a psychiatrist, he knew how to manipulate people's thoughts. In any case, before I left, I signed the agreement to go to hospital.

It took almost another month, before I actually arrived there, as the German Health Insurance system is so slow and complicated and the clinic had a waiting list (though I was put forward for urgency). I was told that I would be there for about 3-4 months; in the end it became almost 6. I instantly took to the rigid programme and the clear rules of the house. The clinic was divided into three sections: an outer section for people who were free to come and go during the day, an inner section with one house for older patients and one for younger ones, who could walk in the extensive grounds, but no further than the fence or the gate, and an innermost section for people who were under constant supervision. I was placed in the inner section.

Seven o'clock was rising time and at quarter past seven we had to be outside for morning exercises. I usually added some jogging, before I went in to wash and dress and go to breakfast. Everybody had their own place in the dining hall and had an obligation to be there for every mealtime, though obviously they could not force us to eat whatever was being dished out. My difficulty with food was not unfounded, as on several occasions during my life I have suffered so badly from vomiting and diarrhoea that my body went into cramp, I lost all feeling in my arms and legs and had difficulty breathing, until I lost consciousness and needed medical attention. Perhaps these experiences led to the two occasions, later interpreted as psychotic episodes, on which I was convinced that people were trying to poison us. Only the intervention of a nurse and the healing power of nature eventually drew me out of it.

After breakfast, a member of staff would give a short "Thought for the day", which I always found very inspiring. This was followed by a time-table of various therapies, like art and craft, movement and dance, music, walks, work, individual and group therapy. During the first two months I also had a lot of time to delve into the clinic's library. I must have studied about 30 books on psychiatry and psychology, taking notes and working things out in my head whilst debating with the authors during my walks in the grounds. Then my psychiatrist assigned me occupational therapy, which involved jobs such as sandpapering jigsaw pieces or sorting out used stamps. I found this so boring that I often thought: "Anyone would go mental after spending two hours in this department." However, sometimes I was allowed to feed the goats or to split fire-wood, which was a bit more to my liking.

On Saturdays, my aunt who lived nearby would pick me up to go hill-walking together, and on Sundays I attended the service in the chapel. One day, in the middle of the sermon, I suddenly had the impression that the ceiling was caving in. It wasn't an entirely new sensation to me, as I often felt uneasy in tall or crowded buildings, but this time it felt so overwhelming that I had to run out. Usually, under the open sky I felt better, but on that morning the fear of being hit by the chapel ceiling was just replaced by the fear of being hit by a tree. Then it wasn't the hitting any longer, but the feeling of my flesh rotting and my hair falling out. Had there been a nuclear disaster somewhere and a poisonous cloud was descending on us? I looked around, but the other people seemed as unconcerned as ever. My fear, however, began to choke me and I was afraid to faint. I tried every technique of distraction that I had taught myself over the years, but nothing worked. In the end I stumbled into the nurse's office and asked for the "tablets against fear", which they had offered me before. I was put on regular medication and found some relief.

Martin's death was one of the topics which came up again and again in my art work and in other therapies. I painted hundreds of pictures of bodies cut up by trains and I made a little coffin and corpse out of clay which I buried outside in the grounds several times. My own suicidal wishes and fears followed on from it and turned out to be closely linked to my loneliness and inability to make friends. My therapist explained this mainly on the basis of my older sisters having been such a close-knit pair and shutting me out, but to me this never seemed to be the foremost reason. After all, my little brother had been able to make friends and there had been people in my life, like my cousins, to whom I could relate quite well. I just didn't understand the way of socialising that most people used naturally. It gave me no pleasure and didn't lead anywhere, but I did feel some kind of bond with people who, like me, didn't fit into our society either. There was, for example, a young physics student who was said to suffer from hallucinations. He often told me the most bizarre stories about his experiments in the laboratory (some of the things, like cloning embryos, actually became reality about ten years later), but he needed help to use the public telephone. Anselm, a Catholic brother who was sometimes sent to split firewood with me, was another interesting person whose presence I enjoyed. He had visions and heard God speak to him like the patriarchs in the Old Testament, but his fellow brothers thought he was suffering from schizophrenia. The girl I shared a room with for much of the time was diagnosed as manic-depressive. She often watched me play with the little town I had made out of clay in the craft room, and I liked her watching, especially when my little people jumped off the roof tops or got smashed by earthquakes. She often gave me a hug afterwards and her embrace never felt suffocating.

The other problem for which I could never find a satisfactory answer was the perception of feelings and thoughts in the objects around me. The bench in the park would smile at me when I approached it and began to cry if I didn't sit down for a minute. The tree was waving its branches as a welcome and couldn't understand why I jogged past instead of climbing up. They all wanted to be acknowledged and valued and involved in my daily routine. It had more or less always been like that. The objects around me had always been alive to me, enriching my lonely world while at the same time exhausting me with their demands. There wasn't an onset of this "mental abnormality". I simply hadn't developed past the stage in which it was seen as normal (the pre-realistic phase or mystical age, according to Piaget). But to my therapist I simply projected my own feelings and thoughts into the objects, as they were easier to deal with outside myself. To her, it was my own cry for attention and value which I heard all around me. As with the aspects of socialising, I could never fully go along with this theory, although to a certain degree it made sense.

However, the main reason for trying to understand what lay behind my problems was to find ways to overcome them. For the first time in my life I was given the time, the space and the help to face up to my fears, pay attention to my feelings in every day encounters and to try out new ways of interacting with situations and people. I learned a lot about my rigidity of thought which often hindered me to find solutions when the one way I had pursued was blocked. It was like finding myself in a dead end, and instead of going on a detour to reach my goal, I just stood there panicking or tried to squeeze past the obstacles, getting hurt or in trouble. Strangely enough, I had always been good at problem-solving in mathematics, but I hadn't been able to transfer these skills to everyday situations.

One such dead end appeared at the beginning of February, when the senior doctor suddenly announced that my time in the clinic was up, as the Health Insurance would only pay for another week or two.

He suggested that I look for a flat and a new job as a gardener and a local psychiatrist, who would see me once in a while. I felt like a patient who had just been cut open for an operation and then been thrown out. There was no way I could go back to gardening and no way could I live on my own. If I was to leave now, I was worse off than when I had first arrived.

I ran into he woods at the edge of the hospital grounds, found an old piece of wire long enough to make a sling and climbed a tree to hang myself. With one end of the wire fixed to a sturdy branch and my head in the sling I got ready to let go. I prayed. I always talked to God about everything. He was and is the only one who really understands me. So I told him that I had no other option. I had nowhere to go. I couldn't cope in this world. In my mind I saw my mother. I felt guilty for causing her pain and grief, but even she couldn't hold me back. I had no choice – or did I? Someone else came to my mind, the one nurse I felt closest to. If I could talk to her, she might be able to help me. So I said to God: "All right, maybe I should give it one more try. I'll climb down and go back to the house and look for Sister Monica. Please, let her be there and show me a way I can go on... or else I'll come back here."

I hid the wire in the leaves under the tree, before I headed back to the ward. On the way I literally bumped into Sister Monica who had just finished her shift and was going home. When she saw the distress that was written all over me, she simply turned back and walked me to her office. I told her what had happened. It was one of the very few occasions in my life that I cried in front of another person. I remember the senior doctor and my therapist coming in. I didn't want them to see me like this. Sister Monica took them aside and talked to them quietly. When they had left, she turned to me and said: "It's all right. You'll have time. Nobody's going to send you away before you're ready. And I'm convinced that God has a place for you in this world, a very special place."

After that I heard no more about the Health Insurance or my time being up, but I was under close observation and had to hand in the wire which I had kept under the tree. My focus shifted from looking at my past to looking at the future. Bible College was no longer an option, neither could I return to my cousin. One day I talked to a patient who had been a residential social worker in a children's home, and I was interested to learn that you didn't need A-levels to enter the course if you had another profession already. I was a qualified gardener after all. The careers adviser gave me a list of colleges for Social Pedagogy and I wrote to those which offered student accommodation. Apart from one, all the courses for the coming session were already full.

The one college which offered me an interview was a small Lutheran institution outside the town where my godmother lived. The hospital gave me leave to travel to the interview. The principal, whose daughter had also suffered mental health problems, felt that having had psychotherapy was a great asset for working with disturbed children, as long as I was on top of my problems. However, what in the end decided the issue of me getting the last place on the course (someone had stepped down) was my cello. When the principal heard that I played the cello, he was over the moon. "This is just the instrument we need for our chamber orchestra", he told me and promptly accepted me on the course.

College wasn't to start before September, though, and this was only March. Then a letter from my cousin arrived, telling me about an American friend of hers who had recently moved near her husband's parent's home in Germany and desperately needed help with her 5 young children. I could start as soon as I was ready. It seemed too perfect to be true. Not only would I be able to speak English with the children (the language of my mind, since my time in Whitby), but I was also hardly any distance away from the college which I was to attend as from September. I was glad that Sister Monica believed in miracles, because this definitely was one. God had provided a special place for me, a way forward which gave me new hope. This time I was the one who brought up the subject of leaving hospital. I was ready to go. Not that all my problems were solved. I was still taking medication to help me cope with my fears, but I had learned many other things which helped me to move on in life.

Chapter 9: On a new path

The day I arrived in my new family, I found myself in the middle of a "pack" of wrestling children. I loved the rough and tumble and the way they accepted me straight away. They had grown up in a hut in the Oregon Mountains, and the half-renovated old mill they inhabited now was an equally adventurous place. I had only been there for a week, when the mother thrust baby Becky into my arms and announced that she needed a holiday. A friend of hers was coming over from the States and they had decided to meet up in Berlin. After all, she hadn't had a holiday for ten years, when her oldest child, Michael, was born. So there I was, suddenly "mother" of five with a laundry full of dirty clothes and a kitchen full of a month's leftovers. The chaos was overwhelming. I wanted to scream and run away. Instead, I started to tidy up.

The father of the children was quite impressed by the change of the house when he came home from his shift at the hospital, where he was training to be a nurse. With the children I mainly played outside to keep the house tidy, and everything would have gone well, if it hadn't been for baby Becky desperately missing her mum. One day she just screamed and screamed and nothing I tried would calm her down. At the end I was ready to throw her against the wall just to silence her. Fortunately, at that moment I heard Michael in the corridor. I stormed out to him with Becky in my arms and told him to take her for a ride in the pram. "And don't come back before this sister of yours is quiet!" Michael did as he was told. Up to this day I don't dare to think about what might otherwise have happened.

The children's father introduced me to the Young Nurses Christian Fellowship (or something like that) where I met Petra. She was a bit of a "weirdo" herself, not quite the typical student nurse, and she often came round on her bicycle. She liked to join in the children's adventures or, when I had time off, to explore the forest with me, where many a time we got lost and, crawling through the undergrowth, couldn't stop laughing our heads off. We rescued frogs together and invented songs and I felt so happy to have a friend of my own age, although I had no clue what I had done to make this happen. Perhaps Petra was simply a gift from God. However, I still needed time to myself, without having to attune to anyone else.

For a few times I saw a psychologist for an hour once a week, which had been a requirement on my release from hospital. The train fare swallowed most of my pocket money and I had to sacrifice my free day. He always asked me to tell him my dreams. Since I was dreaming a lot and waking up several times during the night, I had enough material to keep him happy. One day I told him a dream in which I had been picking up peas from the carpet. The more I picked up, the more were left. Realising how futile my efforts were, my movements became slower and slower until I could no longer bend down and stretch out my hand. It was a nightmare which reminded me so much of my difficulty to perform monotonous tasks, be it in the garden or in the house. Occasionally I did get to the stage where I no longer had the strength to carry out the physical effort required, and yet I could walk or cycle for miles and miles without exhaustion. After I had laid out the dream in every detail, the psychologist looked at me and said: "Come on, you just made this up to impress me." I was shocked. What made him think that? What reason was there for making up stories, when I was asked to tell one of my nightmares? I didn't understand what he was getting at. In fact, I could no longer trust him. On the pretext that the weekly journey was too far and too expensive for me, I declined to make another appointment.

Although I had been looking forward so much to it, my first days at college were far from happy. I was given a room on the ground floor with constant noise floating in from every side – radios, tape recorders, loud voices and door slamming – which I found impossible to cope with. In situations like this, when I was powerless to do anything about the source of the noise and could neither run away from it, I turned the anger against myself. I used to bang my head against the wall or cut my skin with a drawing pin – anything that would release the tension and bring the pain to the surface where it was easier to deal with. Finally I asked the matron if I could move. First she insisted that there wasn't another room available, but seeing my distress, she led me to a little attic room. "Mind you, it gets very cold up here in winter and the window doesn't let in much light", she warned me. I didn't mind the cold and the dark, as long as it was quiet. During the following year I became very fond of my little refuge.

During the first few weeks at college I also had a hot argument with the principal, who was lecturing anthropology. I don't believe that we evolved from monkeys. I still find this an unacceptable racist theory, and unlike other Christians on the course, I couldn't keep my mouth shut. In the end, I bought a book written by a Creationist scientist and persuaded the principal to have a look at it. He did and finally accepted that I had a valid point. From then on, we got on very well and enjoyed many happy hours of harmonious music in the college's chamber orchestra.

Between classes, I usually ran outside to release my physical energy and to breathe in the freedom and fresh air of the open sky. In the beginning, some of the other students made fun of me, especially when I took my wooden walking stick at night and disappeared into the forest. However, once they realised that their teasing didn't put me off, they stopped it, and after a while, one or two others asked if they could join me.
Apart from the usual college time table, those who didn't have A-levels were offered additional classes in Maths and English. It meant a lot of extra work. English was no problem for me, although I still had to

read the required books and hand in my essays. In maths I had more to catch up with, since I hadn't done any higher maths for the past ten years. Trying to copy the teacher's methods of solving problems was useless to me. I had to understand exactly why things worked the way they worked and I could only find this out by spending most of my Saturday mornings poring over my maths jotter until I had grasped the underlying concepts. Then I sometimes came up with quite unorthodox solutions, but as long as they worked, I was allowed to use my methods. Once the maths teacher was quite fascinated by one of my discoveries and wanted to show it to his professor at university.

At the weekends, I went to visit my godmother who did my laundry for me and cooked me a lovely home-grown meal in return for some help in her garden. Twice within our two years at college we were sent away for a block of work experience. Once I spent six weeks in a residential school for children with social and emotional difficulties. I had a hard time there, feeling very lonely and not up to dealing with the cruelty of some of the kids. But there was one particular girl, 13-year old Anna, whom I immediately befriended. We spent hours together in her bizarre world in which I felt a close affinity to her. Although nobody had made the diagnosis then, in retrospect I am certain that all her symptoms, including soiling, sensory issues and hand flapping, were part of Autism or Asperger Syndrome. However, professionals often fail to make this diagnosis in people with good verbal skills and a high IQ.

For my second year at college we had to move into a new building, where I shared a room with a first-year student. We got on amazingly well with each other. I liked her watching me play with the sceno-box, a therapeutic assessment tool, which I often borrowed from the resource room, and we sometimes went into the park together, pretending to be American tourists (she had lived in America before and had a perfect Californian accent) or watching people's reactions to one of us playing care-worker, while the other one acted mentally disabled. It was quite an eye-opener.
I also enjoyed the YMCA youth services in the largest church in town, which was always packed, but sitting or standing at the edge, I felt safe. It was a time when spirituality met with psychology and brought forth a powerful way of addressing deepest human needs and longings, involving music, drama and other forms of art. I always came out of these gatherings full of new hope that life was ultimately good and nothing was impossible for God.

On a regular basis I saw a psychiatrist who supervised my medication. Once he lent me a huge volume of Aaron Beck's Desensitising Programme and gave me some sessions, which were meant to help me overcome my fears and compulsive thoughts. However, they just found other areas of expression.

At the end of my second year at college, "The Silent Cry" was published. One of my long-held dreams had become true: I was an author.

Before I began my probationer year in the children's home, I spent six weeks on an Upward Bound Course in the Austrian Alps. It was run by Canadians, and most people on the course came from North America. The morning after our arrival, we met in the grounds behind the Centre for group building exercises and trust games. Needless to say, I had my problems with this. When one of the instructors announced that everybody had to do the "trust-fall" (= falling backwards from a low wall into the net of arms made by about ten people), I simply took off and didn't stop running until I reached the top of the mountain which overshadowed the village. There I sat down, wondering what to do next. Would I be allowed to stay on the course, although I hadn't done the trust-fall? "He said that we all had to do it…" In the end I was getting cold and hungry and decided to go back to the Centre, as I had nowhere else to go. I was very surprised to see the instructors showing relief when they saw me. One of them took me aside and explained that they would never force me to do something that was beyond me. They just wanted to encourage everyone to try and extend their limits. However, he made me promise never to run away again.
Soon we were packing our rucksacks and went up into the mountains, which had always been my favourite environment. We learned how to use

climbing ropes and to cross glaciers. We spent a night in a deep cave, where I had a panic attack. We repaired footpaths and stayed in mountain huts, and in the evenings I sometimes sneaked off on my own to some exposed rocky ridge and turned into a mountain goat. Being completely fearless of heights, I enjoyed clinging to a tiny ledge and looking into the valley thousands of feet below. Abseiling became a kind of parable for me, and in one of my books I wrote the verse:

Held by the rope of faith,
Connected to God, the Rock,
We can risk steps
Without falling into the abyss.

If I could take the boldness I felt on the heights into my everyday life, nothing would hinder me to achieve my dreams.

The year in the children's home taught me a lot, but it also brought me to the edge of my limits. I could work best with individuals who had a similar mindset to my own. In fact, with a couple of boys I was said to have worked miracles. Unfortunately, most of the time I had to supervise the whole group, which was made up of a dozen children between the age of eight and ten. As long as I could take them outside, building huts in the forest, fishing in the loch or climbing some crags, it was manageable, but trying to teach them table manners or getting them to bed at night often caused mayhem. I never understood how other social workers managed to control the whole lot. I had enough trouble to keep track of three or four. More than that was a crowd to me, and their various voices and movements produced a chaos which I found hard to handle. After a while I began to suffer from chest pain again, which had been quite bad during the months after Martin's death. At times I was crouched on the floor, fighting for breath, as if someone had tied a belt round my chest or put a boulder on top of it. My colleagues finally sent me to see a doctor who, after thorough examination, put it down as stress symptoms. The children's home was well known in town and he said: "You aren't of the material to survive a place like that for long." Since I was homesick for Ireland, I had no intention of staying on after the year anyway. I wrote my thesis on children's play and play therapy and passed my final exams without problems. Through a Christian voluntary organisation I found a job in North Wales – not quite Ireland, but on the way to it – and exactly ten years after I had left my mother's house in search of a home on the Celtic Fringe, I set out again with still the same objective.

Chapter 10: The Quest goes on

My post was in a Residential Rehabilitation Centre
for women who had suffered from addiction, abuse
and mental health problems, and their children. I
worked alongside Alison, a young psychologist from
Glasgow, who shared my love for the outdoors. While
she was mainly working with the adults, my
responsibility were the children.
With one 5-year-old boy I formed a special bond. In
the beginning he was very immature and withdrawn
and never smiled. The two of us spent hours at the
beach, running in and out the waves, chasing each
other with seaweed and finding all sorts of treasure.
We built sandcastles where a terrible giant lived who
was always defeated and destroyed at the end. Our
walks became longer, as his legs grew stronger,
taking us to the cliffs and the rhododendron jungle
and many other fascinating places. He slowly lost his
scowl and sadness. He began to smile and to laugh
and to show enthusiasm, as if he had woken from a
long dark dream. For me it was almost like
befriending and setting free a part of myself. His
loneliness and sadness was my own, and so were his
smiles and his laughter. Most people, when meeting a
child who draws away from them, either keep a
distance or try to coax it closer to themselves. Very
few make the effort to leave their own realm and
draw alongside the child, waiting for him or her to let
them in. Perhaps my own experience has given me
the advantage of doing this naturally.

The little boy changed immensely, but his mother couldn't cope with his change and resented the special relationship we had formed. Her own difficulties worsened, until she went back to hospital. A few weeks later, her son was picked up by his father and grandmother. I never saw him again. This and the fact that the Centre had funding problems made me decide to take up another voluntary post, this time in Scotland. Alison, who had shared many a hairy adventure in Snowdonia National Park with me, insisted that once I was in Scotland, I would never want to leave again.

Although during the first ten days of my stay at the Glencoe Outdoor Centre it was raining non-stop and I saw nothing of the surrounding mountains, Alison proved to be right. I fell in love with the country and have lived here for the past fifteen years, changing my nationality and learning the native Gaelic language to take a clear stance where I belong.

Once the mountains emerged from the clouds, I felt a desperate longing to escape to the heights. On my own or with others from the Centre, I spent most of my free time climbing the steep rock faces, balancing along narrow ridges and navigating through white-outs to *bag* another Munro. I became proficient in handling ice axe and crampons, ropes and pitons, map and compass, assessing avalanche danger and how to survive a night in a snow hole. This was the "real" life in contrast to the "artificial" life down in the glen. Even relating to people became much simpler up there on the mountain, as the instinct for survival bound us together in a natural way. In the end it was due to my recurring back problem that I had to leave outdoor education. I spent nine months at Bible College (finally!) in search of further direction for my life. All the time I kept writing books, mainly adventure novels for children and teenagers, which were published in Germany. Although the royalties were not great, it enabled me to finance my studies, both at college and later at university.

My time at Bible College was rather disappointing. I enjoyed the academically challenging subjects, like theology and philosophy, but I found most of the other classes rather boring. Almost every week some mission society gave a presentation, advertising themselves as the most important one to join or support. I found this very confusing. Their arguments were well founded, but how could each of them be the most important one? Actually, I applied to a couple of mission societies that were looking for children's workers, but as soon as they heard of my mental health background, they turned me down.

My greatest disappointment at college was the lack of fellowship. Although I often withdrew to remote places, I was at the same time desperately hungry for human contact. I resurrected and refined my vision of the *Celtic Christian Community*, where people would live creatively together, playing music, sharing work and play, discussing deep questions and building the Kingdom of God. However, at Bible College people rarely had time for such activities, as they were always busy with their studies, prayer groups and all sorts of outreach. Of course, there were spontaneous ways of socialising and relationships were formed which later led to marriage. But these things were closed to me, as I never understood the art of it.

When my time at college was drawing to an end, the question of "what next?" was looming high again. Change and uncertainties always caused me a great deal of anxiety, and yet it was something I constantly had to face up to. After much searching and prayer, I was finally offered a job in a Christian Day Care Centre for children (Nursery and After School Care) in Banchory/Aberdeenshire. The family in charge of it was extremely kind and open-minded. They shared their house and their life with me, as if I was one of their kin. I had only been there for a week, when they invited me to the Highland Games. As so often, when faced with a spontaneous decision I declined. Once I got used to the idea, I asked if I could join them after all. We had a great day out.

Half way through the year, the family left and the management of the Centre passed into the hands of a business woman from London. Her ideas constantly clashed with my working practice, which made the following months very stressful for both of us. By then I was living with the cook and her family, who had kindly offered me lodgings. Soon I found myself job hunting again. The old chest pains returned and I felt very depressed, wondering if I was ever to find a place where I fit in.

During a weekend conference held at the Bible College I attended a lecture on Celtic Christianity given by the Head of the Celtic Department of

Aberdeen University. The subject fascinated me, and the principal of the Bible College made the suggestion of taking up further studies. In the end I enrolled in the full-time degree course in Celtic and Gaelic Studies, taking on more work for my German publisher to have the necessary funding, as I didn't get a grant.

The day came, when I moved into the Halls of Residence in Aberdeen shortly after my 31st birthday. For some people the path of life is not straight forward, but as long as it leads us towards our goals, the extra steps are not wasted.

Chapter 11: At University

I was already wearing foam earplugs, a walkman with soothing music on top and was burying my head under my pillow, but the noise from the flat beneath ours still penetrated through all of it. "Dom, dom, dom…" I felt as if I was being pounded with a sledge hammer. I tried to distract myself by reading one of my history books, but my mind wasn't fooled. Asking the lads to turn their music down was a waste of time. Escaping to the kitchen didn't help either. I knew that any minute I would freak out and either start cutting myself or banging my head against the wall. The thing was, this noise went on day and night. I simply couldn't take anymore. What was I to do? When I had applied for a place in the Halls of Residence, I received a long list of rules for behaviour which ensured me that it was the right place for me to live. However, I soon found out that many students completely ignored these rules, and the porters and wardens were either powerless or unwilling to enforce them. Those who suffered did so in silence. The rest just kept doing what they liked.

I had a terrible time in my first year's accommodation, and I soon took to spending the weekends out in the country, either with the cook's family in Banchory or with the Nicol family, whose youngest son had been in my nursery group and who lived in a remote forestry lodge. There I would unwind and catch up on sleep, which I had missed during the week.

The Celtic Department was small enough for students and lecturers soon to come to know each other. I enjoyed the Gaelic classes, although it wasn't an easy language to learn, and I was very interested in Celtic and Scottish history. My first essay, which my tutor called a dissertation because of its length and amount of research, was about the history of the church in Scotland. For most of my essays I was awarded outstanding marks, despite the fact that they were either handwritten or painstakingly typed on my old typewriter.

The Chaplaincy soon became a refuge for me. It was a quiet place to study during the day and to eat my lunch when the weather didn't allow a picnic outside. I joined the Student Christian Movement, the meditative Taize Prayer group and the Iona Community Morning Prayers led by the lady chaplain. However, I was still suffering from depression, anxiety, attacks of chest pain and obsessive/compulsive thoughts which took a lot of energy to keep under control. I hadn't taken any medication since leaving Germany, apart from a recent course of beta-blockers to ease the chest pain, which was apparently linked to hyperventilation. Finally, my GP arranged for a meeting with a psychologist. Once more I had to fill in a long questionnaire, but I was careful to play things down a bit. The lady who interviewed me was very efficient.

Although I never looked at her face, I had a sense that her expression didn't give away anything that lay behind it. In the end she suggested anti-depressant medication and some sessions of cognitive therapy. I was afraid of the medication, and cognitive therapy hadn't done anything for me in the past. As soon as I had told her this, she got up and announced that I would have to see somebody else. I think I made her angry by not embracing her suggestions, but then it wasn't my fault if she couldn't cope with disagreement.

The next day I was seen by a psychiatrist. Whilst sitting in the waiting room, I heard him talking to the nurses about something funny his son had done at school. I instantly liked his openness and relaxed manners, which were so different from the cold efficiency of the psychologist. It was easy to talk to him, and when he wasn't clear about something, he simply asked for clarification. He was interested in my compulsive thoughts and my struggle with obsessions. I told him about my sensitivity to noise and my problems with socialising. I also shared my longing to be part of a Spiritual Community, whereupon he replied that he was currently living in one. He won my trust, and in the end I even agreed to try anti-depressants, as long as they didn't cause any detrimental side effects. He gave me a follow-up appointment, before we parted.

For the next couple of weeks, the hour we had spent together became like a tape which I played over and over in my mind. I knew that I had finally come across a person who met me where I was and who had the ability to accompany me into the depth and help me to climb out of it. If he was to become my therapist, my prayers of the past seven years (since leaving hospital) had found an answer. Since he had shown an interest in my work as an author, I wrote a little book for him: *The World under the Sea*. I wasn't sure whether I would have the courage to give it to him, as giving and receiving presents has always been difficult for me, but I took it along to my next appointment anyway.

We met in a different room at the Student Health Service and I felt very nervous, as there was so much at stake. When he mentioned that he could not take me on for psychotherapy, my heart sank and for an instant I simply froze. However, there was nothing I could do about it and since I wasn't going to see him again, I might as well give him the book. I thrust it into his hands and once more focussed on my feet. For what seemed like ages a silence hung over the room, in which I could hear my heart pounding against my chest. Then he took a deep breath and said: "Well, I think I'll find a way to take you on for psychotherapy after all."

I looked up, not quite making sense of his words. He nodded, his thoughts still working rapidly behind his forehead. Then he gave me an appointment at the hospital and wrote down some instructions for where to find him. I took the note from him, still unsure if this was really happening. He must have sensed my doubts, because when I got up he asked me if I could feel the ground under my feet. Yes, I could feel it.

This was real. My prayers had been answered. I went home like in a daze, more hopeful that I had been for a long time.

Chapter 12: Someone to meet me where I am

For the following three years we met at the hospital for an hour every week, apart from the months which I had to spend away on placements and a time when David's wife was seriously ill or when they were on holidays. As I mentioned before, he picked me up where I was and allowed me to use the tools which suited me best to express myself. I had never found it easy to identify my feelings, let alone to put them into words. Yet faced with a piece of paper and paint, they would express themselves effortlessly, bypassing the mind.

David was there to observe and to reflect back to me what he saw, whereby I learned more and more to recognise what I felt and the causes behind it. He also drew my attention to the fact that in my paintings and drawings people never had faces. In fact, I have always found it hard to look at people's faces, finding it somewhat intrusive, and even when I force myself to keep eye-contact, I don't really see their face but rather the outline of it. I usually recognise people by their hair and their posture and gait. On the other hand, when I meet people out of their familiar context, I often don't recognise them at all, or I see someone with a certain posture and hairstyle and mistake him or her for someone else. As this can be very embarrassing, I often close out people from my visual field altogether. David encouraged me to observe others, not just animals and children, but people of my own age. So I went down to the beach, watching the surfers getting ready for the sea, but their faces often seemed to betray their true emotions or else I didn't get the message right.

Apart from drawing and painting, I let inner conflicts and fears come to the surface in the form of stories, whether written, told or played. In fact, each of my published books contains a lot of my own experiences, not only the adventures they describe, but more so the personality and inner struggles of the characters. Once my German publisher asked me to write a Celtic historical novel, which took me the whole summer between my first and second year at university and many more months of previous research and later editing and typing (I always write by hand). I stayed with a friend on the Isle of Lewis, who had a little backroom with a view across the moor and the mountains. I would sit there for hours, writing away, and when Fiona looked in to offer me a cup of tea or simply to check if I was still alive, she appeared to me like someone from a different world. I was Ronan who had just run away from the druid or been shipwrecked on Iona or paddled across Loch Ness to see King Brude. Even when after a day's work at my desk I allowed myself to run across the moor, I was still Ronan, still in that role, just as I had been Blue Bird or the Vietnamese war orphan when I was a child. Perhaps that is how every convincing author works, like every good actor. In any case, David never seemed to tire of my stories and knew how to use them to help me understand myself better.

The second year at university, which was also the first year of our therapy sessions, I stayed in nicer Halls of Residence, though also more expensive. Apart from one girl on our corridor, we all got on splendidly with each other. Rachel, who came from America, asked me one day to accompany her in her music exam, reciting a piece for trumpet and cello which she had composed herself. It took quite a bit of practice together, but in the end she passed with flying colours and the professor invited me to play in the university orchestra, which I did for a year.

With another girl, Elaine, I often went to the swimming pool, playing duck rescue (I had found some rubber ducks which had fallen off a lorry) and water gymnastics. And Claire, who later became a countryside ranger, received many a dead (or not so dead) creature from us to aid her studies. They all rejoiced with me when my first book was published in English, though I never received any royalties for it. To a certain degree I experienced the Community life which I had always longed for. I felt accepted and belonging.

David also told me about the Findhorn Community which he and his family were part of. He often mentioned that I would fit in there, so I finally booked a place on an *Experience Week*. Matthew, my good old fluff-dog, accompanied me, as he always does when an overnight stay is involved. One of the workshop leaders (or foculisers), Corinna, took to him immediately and in doing so opened my heart to her. It turned out to be a very intense and valuable week for me: the group games and circle dancing, meditations, outings and times of sharing, in fact the whole atmosphere of the place made me feel accepted with all my oddities.

One night, however, while we were gathered in a circle for sharing time, I felt very restless and the noise of the rock music coming from the kitchen reverberated in my head until it seemed ready to burst. I asked the foculisers to do something about it, but they insisted that the kitchen crew needed the buzz to get on with their work. Since I couldn't put up with it, I decided to leave the room. Had I been able to go for a run in the forest, as I intended to, I am sure I would have calmed down. However, I was stopped and confronted about it, and with the rock music still blaring in the background, the only temporary relief I could find was by cutting myself. I took a drawing pin from the notice board and slashed it again and again across my forearm. Once I had started, I couldn't stop. All the stored-up tension was released in the scratching of the pin and the trickle of blood that followed. I no longer noticed the world around me. I was absolutely captivated by the little drawing pin, which seemed to have taken on a life of its own, dancing across my skin and laughing at the picture it drew on my arm.

When Corinna came back from the cloakroom, she was shocked. She took the pin off me, but I couldn't stop laughing. I didn't feel the pain, perhaps because I have always had a very high pain threshold or my brain simply couldn't identify the feeling at that moment. Corinna led me outside to someone who said he was a friend of David. I can't remember what else he said, but his voice was calming while I wiped the blood off my arm with a cloth someone else had given me. Meanwhile Corinna was on the phone to David, who must have assured her not to panic about the incident. In fact, soon everything was all right again, but unfortunately it had consequences later when I applied for other workshops. My memories of *Experience Week* and especially of Corinna will always be precious to me.

In my third year at university I once more had trouble with accommodation, as I had opted for one of the cheapest student flats. Twice I had to move within the street until I finally shared a house with one of the girls from our former corridor. It was an extremely cold winter and the flat was freezing, as we couldn't afford to heat it properly. Instead, we sealed the windows with cardboard to keep out the drought, went to bed with woollen socks and balaclava under a pile of blankets, ate breakfast with gloves on and defrosted under the showers of the university swimming pool which was free for students. Needless to say, we were never ill that winter. Who would have wanted to stay in bed in conditions like that!

The most important question that year was about career options. When I embarked on Celtic Studies, it was out of interest in the subject, but now that my funds were running out and the course was nearing its end, I had to consider what path to take next. For a while I explored the possibility of a museum's career, but employment opportunities were very scarce.

Instead, from every side came the call for teachers in Gaelic medium education, and after tutoring one morning a week in a Gaelic Unit for a term, I decided to go down that route. I was one of the 15% of applicants who were offered a place on the PGCE (Primary) course at Northern College, but in the end I realised that I wasn't confident enough in Gaelic and preferred to do my training in English speaking classes.

Since I had been on *Experience Week*, the world I withdrew into on my walks and at night was often filled with scenes, real or imagined, from Findhorn. Over and over again I relived one of the group games, which I had first shied away from until a skilled facilitator somehow drew me in. I don't know what "magic powers" she employed, but at the end I was part of the "big hug" (though on the outskirts) without the usual panic. The memory of Corinna's hand on my back whenever I felt anxious, was another source for many a story while I was drifting off to sleep. Part of me was longing to feel her loving touch again, and it was an area which I more and more explored in my sessions with David. Deep down I had always been hungry for loving (non-sexual) physical contact, but what had been offered, I couldn't bear; just as I had always ached for friends, yet felt the need to withdraw from people. It seemed so paradoxical, as I was trying to make sense of it. One thing I discovered, especially amongst fellow students at the chaplaincy and during other Findhorn workshops, was that only certain types of adults, those who were able to give freely without seeking fulfilment for their own needs, felt safe enough for me to receive physical kindness from, and people like that are unfortunately very rare. As soon as I sense any kind of selfish motive behind someone's approach, I instinctively withdraw. This is not to say that children and animals never have selfish motives when giving or looking for physical contact. But perhaps their needs are different, of an innocent nature and more openly acknowledged. I don't know. I will need more time to understand these complex issues. Meanwhile I treasure the experiences which have been acceptable and enjoyable for me.

The teacher training year was in many ways one of the worst times of my life. After being used to outstanding marks at university, I suddenly found myself in trouble with almost every lecturer. Having strong convictions about education and not disguising my disagreement, brought about many clashes with staff and students, but just as many of these were simply due to misunderstandings. Whereas at university critical thinking had been essential, at college you had to favour the lecturers opinion, use the right jargon and present a neat copy of your assignment with as many special features as the computer could afford. For much of the time we were just learning how to deal with the paperwork of the profession, which seemed more important than the children. Daily plans, group plans, lesson plans, weekly plans, forward plans, year plans – and not to forget the evaluation of each of those plans, in addition to assessments and report cards sometimes made me wonder when teachers were actually free to teach. What I really needed to know about children and how they learn and develop, I had picked up at Social Work College, during the two semesters of medical psychology at university and most of all by reflecting on my own childhood and the children I came in contact with.

Thus equipped, I went into the various schools for my placements, where I was usually left alone with the class, while the teacher took the much needed time to bring her paperwork (all those plans) up to date. It was an immensely stressful year, especially as part of the course was delivered on the Dundee campus, where I was lodging with a teacher, and part of it in Aberdeen, where I stayed with the university chaplain and her family. David was still there for me most weeks, helping me to make sense of life and to understand myself better. But I knew that our sessions were coming to an end. He told me long in advance that he was going to move to London to work with the Psychosynthesis Trust, and finally the day came when we had to say good bye. I could hear my chair in his office scream with grief long after I had left. It was one of the most painful bereavements of my life. David had met me in my world, shared my confusion and my pain and shared his time and his tools to turn them into deeper understanding and joy. His voice and his being will always live on in me.

David's departure couldn't have come at a worse time, as it coincided with my graduation from college and a flood of unsuccessful job applications throughout Scotland. On top of this came the sudden rejection from a Findhorn workshop which I had pinned great hopes on. The lady who ran it, having learned about my past, was afraid that she couldn't cope with me. At that time I was staying with the Nicol family, who provided me with a home base in their forestry lodge during my years as a student and beyond. When they went away on holidays, I stayed behind with good old Mizpah, the Labrador, writing more job applications and another book, which my German publisher promptly rejected.

It was one of the wettest summers Scotland had ever seen. Nevertheless, I cycled to church every Sunday, where one elderly lady was particularly kind and understanding to me. However, my mood was getting lower and my hope of finding a job and a meaningful life dwindled away. Once again I found myself in a cul-de-sac with no way out but through death. Although I still had sufficient medication from my former GP, I went to the local doctor and asked for more. Together with some packets of painkillers I was sure I had enough to end this life, provided I could get it all down. I waited for the day on which the family was due back, so that Mizpah would be cared for. My plan was to go deep into the forest, swallow the tablets and wait for the end, while Mizpah was waiting in the house for the Nicols to come back. I wrote a letter to David, addressing it to the Findhorn Community, to ask his forgiveness for giving up. Then I prayed, begging God to forgive me, since I could see no other option. I simply couldn't go on any longer. "Unless you do a miracle to hold me back, I'm on my way now..." I had hardly spoken the words when I heard voices outside. Some of the Home Farm children had cycled up and were calling for me. It had to be at that moment. I got up and let them in, giving them a drink and some biscuits and pretended to listen to their chatter. They were so full of life. We had climbed trees together and tumbled on the grass with the dogs snatching at our toes. I don't know, but when they left, something had changed in me. I couldn't go off and kill myself anymore. Some of their love for life must have rubbed off on me and rekindled a spark of hope that there had to be a way forward for me in this world.

In fact, a couple of weeks later, thanks to David, I was allowed to take part in another Findhorn workshop where I met an immensely supportive group, in particular a Swiss girl who approached me on the first night with the words: "You look very sad. May I give you a hug?" Her embrace felt safe and warm, and for the rest of the week she stayed by my side, helping me to regain the will to live. Afterwards I spent a week in a retreat house on the Isle of Iona, where I read an amazing book: "The Call" by David Spangler. It renewed my faith that God has a purpose for every life He creates, and by attuning to Him we can work out this purpose together. At the end of the week, two options had opened up for me: I could go to the Gaelic College on the Isle of Skye for a year (they offered me a full bursary) to become fluent enough to take up a post in Gaelic medium education.

Or I could go to Edinburgh, where the Council was very short of supply teachers, and embark on an evening course in Steiner Education with the goal of one day getting a job at the Steiner School of the Findhorn Community. After much thought and prayer, I chose the second option. With new hope I returned to the house in the forest to pack what I needed and to get ready for a new stage on my journey through life.

Chapter 13: The Start of a Career

For the first few months in Edinburgh I was lodging with an elderly lady who had connections to the Steiner School. Her house was very quiet, which was so important to me, but as time went on she demanded more and more house work from me in addition to the rent I paid. She also accused me of things, like leaving the fridge door ajar, which she had done herself. Once she made me feel so awful that I went up into my little room, pulled a bin bag over my head and sealed it at the neck to suffocate myself. However, that bag must have been made of breathable plastic, as after twenty minutes I was no nearer to death and decided to take it off. The stress of looking around for accommodation began again.

In the beginning, the course at the Steiner School was very enjoyable, although I frequently got into trouble for not taking matters seriously enough. There were, for example, the painting sessions. I loved the Steiner art of smearing colours on a wet piece of paper to create dreamlike scenes. But at times my enthusiasm didn't stay within the acceptable limits and my paintings flowed over onto the table, my apron and perhaps the floor. Twice I couldn't stop laughing about the effect until I was thrown out.
Eurhythmy was another activity which had the potential to carry me away. This is a form of translating words into movement and acting out verses of poetry, usually in a group. Since I have

always had a problem with slow movements, I often found myself sailing through the gym like a rocket rather than a fairy, getting the words all muddled up or simply repeating the last line over and over again, as it was all I could remember.

However, what expelled me from the course after the first term was neither Art, nor Eurhythmy, but Steiner's philosophy. I studied it and wrestled with it probably in greater depth than any of the other students to the point that our lecturer couldn't cope with my arguments during our discussions. She accused me of not being receptive enough for Steiner's ideas, whereas I argued that they were contradicting themselves and didn't make sense. So this finally put an end to my attempt of becoming a Steiner School teacher.

Meanwhile I was busy teaching in local Primary Schools. I usually phoned the Education Office the day before and they told me where my services were required. If there was no work available, I was still packed and ready by eight o'clock in the morning, waiting for an emergency call from one of the schools. It was the toughest start for any probationer teacher, but for someone like me, who is so anxious of the unknown and unpredictable, it must have caused double the amount of stress. Equipped with my street plan, I would find the shortest route to school within minutes and zoom off on my bicycle like a fire fighter or ambulance driver. In fact, we supply teachers soon earned the grand name

"Emergency Educational Specialists", although we were not added to the 999 call.

Many of the pupils I taught took advantage of the fact that I didn't know their names and routines and some frankly greeted me with the words: "We don't do any work for supply teachers" or ignored me altogether. In addition, every head teacher had different priorities and expectations, and more than once I was mistakenly called out to an infant class and ended up in the upper stages or vice versa. Some classes only needed me for a day, some for a week, a month or even a whole term. Some schools asked me back again and again, while others complained about me to the Education Office, usually stating that I couldn't keep discipline. Well, amongst teachers it was called "crowd control", especially in areas where the children were mostly left to their own devices at home and couldn't see why at school they were expected to submit to adults.

Many a time I cried out to God: "I can't do this job!" and was ready to give up. But what was I to do instead? Two friends of mine, both teachers in Edinburgh, gave me a lot of support and encouragement. There were also many children who showed me with pictures and little "love"-letters that they appreciated who I was and what I was doing. And of course, I learned from experience and soon found out what was important to establish first. I also knew that in order to keep the overview of the whole class, I had to teach class lessons. So I soon came up with certain standard lessons, like "How an author works", which I could adapt for any class between P3 and P7. For the infants I brought my ukulele along to sing together and my storyteller puppet and other treasures, and for the older ones I made up problem-solving exercises and a general-knowledge-quiz.

I learned that some children very easily picked up my level of confidence and acted accordingly. So I tried to boost my self-esteem by scaling mountains at the weekend and by having another book published in English at my own cost. Needless to say, I never retrieved a penny, but it did give me great joy at the time and I even had a two-page interview in the local newspaper, which made me "famous" for a few days. Meanwhile the contact to my German publisher dried up. During my time in Edinburgh I wrote three more collections of short-stories I was asked for, but I found it increasingly difficult to write in German and after over thirty published titles, I think I had exhausted both myself and my audience.

After I had given up the Steiner School course, I went to evening classes at the Salisbury Centre. I enjoyed painting, pottery and circle dancing and tried tai-chi and meditations, but didn't have the necessary patience for it. I met many new people with common interests, yet as usual the contacts didn't extend beyond the organised activities.

When I moved into a shared flat at Tollcross, I had to enrol with another GP. This doctor became a great help to me during the coming years. One thing he did almost at once was to put me in touch with the psychotherapy department. I had just got through the seemingly endless medicals required by the Council to confirm that I was fit for the job. I was tired of interviews and weary of personal questions about my mental health, yet when I finally got an appointment with the psychotherapist, the meeting was quite refreshing. He put me on a waiting list for group therapy, although the prospect of sitting in a circle for an hour and a half talking about one's problems didn't appeal to me at all.

A few months later I went for an appointment with the group therapist. She listened patiently, while I was explaining the various reasons why this therapy would not work for me. Then there followed silence, only interrupted by my trembling knees (something I have no control over). Suddenly she said: "I get the impression that you are very sad." I was stunned. How could she sum up the essence of my feelings so accurately, when all I had done was to explain my difficulties sitting still for any length of time and listening and talking to strangers? I didn't know what to reply, but deep down I felt drawn to her as I had felt drawn to David, someone who was able to see through my shell and wasn't afraid to link up with the wounded child in its prison.

So eventually I joined the group, and for the next two years it became the highlight of the week, although I could never sit still in that chair. What gave me most was not the other group members, nor our conversations which I have largely forgotten. It was rather the care and acceptance I sensed coming from Kay, the therapist, which I carried away into my day dreams. Often, while walking in the Pentland Hills outside the city or cycling out along the canal, I imagined meeting her, recalling her voice and her words. Sometimes I "saw" her in the congregation, when I played my cello in the Praise Band at church. I tried to figure out where she lived and if she had family. David had often spoken about his wife and his children and his Community. It had made him more real to me, and in the same way I wanted Kay to be more real and not confined to one room and an hour and a half each week. All my life I have struggled with the distinction between reality and imagination. "Did I make this person up or does he/she really exist? Was this a story or a true event? Is the chair telling me its feelings or am I projecting my feelings into it?" Questions such as these are almost daily on my mind. At times I would even find myself wondering whether I am really standing in front of the class, watching that teacher with my voice and my looks talking to the children, as if she had nothing to do with me. Perhaps I have spent too much time in my own little world, or maybe some part of my brain didn't develop in the usual way, causing thoughts and feelings which alienate me from myself and the world around me. Or, as David sometimes speculated, there are a lot more dimensions to life and only a few people have the natural gift (or curse) to tap into them.

One weekend, whilst staying in a youth hostel, I met a man who turned out to be a homeopath and showed an interest in the Gaelic lore connected with herbs and healing which I had come across during my studies. A contact began and soon developed into a friendship. We often met up in some remote youth hostel to go hill-walking together and talk about nature, faith and life in general. When I needed my own space for a while, I just walked ahead, but I also enjoyed a hug and a cuddle as long as I didn't touch his bare skin.

Despite many more job applications and interviews, I was still doing supply work and began to doubt that I would ever get any further in my teaching career. So when Norman mentioned an interest in marriage, I gave it serious contemplation. I imagined a little house in the country, where I would bring up some children in a happy and healthy way, growing vegetables and keeping chickens and perhaps a cow for fresh milk. No more emergency call-outs, no more crowd control, no more arguments with landladies and flatmates. It appealed to me apart from the prospect of having to share a bed with a man. One weekend we were visiting the Nicols in their forestry lodge, where Julie was watching us closely. At the end she took me aside and asked: "Do you really love Norman in a physical way, like kissing..."

"Yuk! Not kissing" The very thought made me feel sick. "Well", Julie went on, "that's the difference between marriage and friendship, you share your body with each other."

Of course, she was right. The whole idea had been more of an escape from supply teaching and city life than a call of genuine love. Poor Norman was very disappointed when I told him so and still kept hoping for a deeper relationship until I felt trapped and broke up the contact altogether. At least I would know for the future that marriage wasn't for me and made it clear to anyone who might harbour false hopes.

As a miraculous answer to prayer, I finally got a class for a whole year, which allowed me to finish my probation and become a fully registered teacher. However, my dream by then was to work with small groups of children with special needs. I had done some supply work in Special Schools and in Language Units for children on the Autistic Spectrum. So I enrolled in an evening course in Learning Support and Special Educational Needs, which meant that I had to miss some of my valuable group therapy sessions. For the course I read several books on Autism and was surprised how much of it applied to me, yet in other areas, like language acquisition, I didn't fit the diagnosis, so I ruled it out.

In the spring of my year with the P4 class, I took part in an expedition to Nepal to climb a couple of trekking peaks in the vicinity of Mount Everest. Since my childhood, I had read so many expedition accounts that it had become one of my ambitions to experience the Himalayas for myself. The long flight was one of the major hurdles. Once that was put behind us, I fought with the intense cold, nausea and cerebral oedema (High Altitude Sickness) and with deep loneliness. Apart from the ever-present God and my little stuffed dog Matthew, I couldn't share my thoughts and feelings with anyone in the group, though I had great respect for the Sherpas and their good nature and decency. However, I managed to reach both peaks, though one of them almost delirious. It was an unforgettable experience and made me much bolder in my future climbs in the Alps and in Scotland.

Although the head teacher would have liked me to continue in my post, the Education Office put a new probationer in instead, so that I was once more forced to do short-term supply. Just then, our therapist announced that the group would be coming to an end before Christmas, due to time constraints. This hit me hard and yet, as before, it set me free to explore other areas of Scotland where my life and career might have a better chance to advance.

I had some major problems with one of my flatmates and for the first time in my life the idea of living on my own began to appeal to me. My parents offered me some money towards buying property and with my frugal life style I had saved up some myself. However, prices in Edinburgh were so high that I couldn't afford even the tiniest and shabbiest flat. During an Easter break in Glen Affric my eyes fell on Inverness. The town was a better size for me than Edinburgh and property prices were considerably lower. It was surrounded by mountains, close to the Findhorn Community and I might even be able to make use of my Gaelic. Finally I found an ex-Council flat in a quiet cul-de-sac which was just affordable for me, and with the generous help of friends I made the move at the beginning of the summer holidays. The four years in Edinburgh lay behind me. Whatever the future would hold, I didn't know.

Chapter 14: The Answer

It took me two months to clean out the flat, paper and paint the walls, lay new carpets and get rid of more than half of the previous owner's furniture. I enjoyed having the whole place to myself and keeping it as simple and orderly as I liked it. I had a little garden where I grew vegetables and planted a cherry tree. First I got on well with my neighbours, especially the older ones. One of them offered to trim curtains for me on her sewing machine and arranged for me to take her daughter's young Labrador for walks. Later the picture changed, when one of the old ladies died and a young family moved in who regularly had the police round because of domestic violence.

During the first few months I was back on short-term supply. I even taught regularly in a Gaelic medium class, but I felt far from confident. The Special School called me out again and again and so did another school with a high number of children with special needs.

I published another book, this time under a Scottish synonym, and once more lost a lot of money. Through an advertisement at the library, I joined the local NSF (National Schizophrenia Fellowship). I had been questioning whether my mental health problems might fall into this category, but although I had experienced psychotic episodes, my wider personality did not at all fit the picture of schizophrenia. Even my depression was so unlike other people's, who want to curl up in bed and cry. I have always been so full of physical energy that I couldn't stay in bed even when I had badly injured my leg and was supposed to rest it. And as for mania, I certainly feel great elation when I stand on top of a mountain, but I am always aware that I have to get myself down again. In other words: I never float on clouds.

Finally I was able to stay with one class for five months, and after that I was offered a job share in the Special School and Learning Support in another school for the other half of the week, both for a whole year. And this is where I met Brandon (name changed). I had already been acquainted with him before, but now he became one of my regular pupils. At age seven, he was keenly studying medical books, constantly asking the most sophisticated questions, but he didn't know how to play with other children. Since he had a diagnosis of Asperger Syndrome, I borrowed Tony Attwood's book on the subject to be better informed. What I read took my breath away. On almost every page I found a description of myself. There were firstly the sensory aspects, being overwhelmed by audio, visual and tactile stimuli. The noise from my upstairs neighbour, which other people might have been able to tolerate, eventually forced me to move again, this time to a tiny detached cottage. Then there were the already mentioned problems I have with selective hearing. Even with the utmost concentration I cannot follow a conversation when several people around me are talking at the same time. I read about the intolerance of tactile closeness, like skin against skin, certain types of clothing and certain human proximity. The stress and confusion caused by visual over-stimulation or changes in the environment. The preferred sameness of food, music, routines etc. and the need for regular solitude. The literal interpretation of what is said and the difficulty of wrapping up facts instead of barging them out. The inability to identify and appropriately express emotions and to understand the art and meaning of small talk. Thinking conversations out loud or replaying them over and over again. Even the lack of a defined accent (I am always pleased when people think that I come from the Western Isles).

And, of course, the social issues: the difficulty interpreting social cues, the lack of feeling peer pressure, empathy only for people on my own wavelength (although this is probably true for most of us), inflexibility to react to spontaneous situations (which caused me a lot of stress with short-term supply work), my strong moral code and sense of justice and the fact that my social contacts have always been entirely based on shared interests. All this stared me in the face when I read Tony Attwood's description of Asperger Syndrome. There was my delayed emotional maturity (at times I am still the 12-year old boy), my high need for simplicity and order, my rituals and obsessions and certain interests to the exclusion of all else (at the moment this is Polar Exploration and the North-West-Passage), my concrete visual thinking, like the colours of days and months, and the withdrawal into my imaginary world, the profound loneliness and constant anxiety – it was all there in this book and as a living example in little Brandon.

When I put the book down, it was only to pick up a dozen others on the subject. Some were biographies, while others were medical, psychological or educational guide books. Obviously, every person is unique and therefore no two people with Asperger Syndrome are exactly the same. For a while I found the diagnostic criteria of physical clumsiness hard to accept. I would never consider myself clumsy whilst swinging from branch to branch in the trees or scrambling through narrow gullies up a mountain ridge, and neither did Brandon appear clumsy to me. On the other hand, we both have difficulty with slow movements and tend to walk on tiptoe when anxious or excited. Once I was thrown out of a Circle Dance group for dancing too wildly and breaking someone's toe. Also, some of my fine motor skills have always been rather awkward, like using scissors or knives or the computer mouse. Perhaps the word "clumsy" means different things to different people (as is the case with so much of our language!).

The main thing for me is to have found an explanation that encompasses all aspects of my mental health problems and the way I experience the world, while the heading "Developmental Disorder" makes it clear that this has always been part of me and the cause must lie somewhere in my brain. When I shared this at the assessment with the clinical psychologist, she confirmed my diagnosis and praised me for all I had achieved in spite of it. At the time, I took it for a formal diagnosis, but I was later to learn that to make it official was a rather complicated procedure. I wonder what makes many professionals so reluctant to acknowledge this condition. However, the psychologist put me in contact with the local Autistic Society, which gave me access to a wide range of literature on the subject.

At the age of forty, I got my first permanent job for 3 ½ days per week doing Learning Support in Brandon's school, thanks to the head teacher who did not put me through a formal interview, after having watched me for a year working with the children and appreciating what I did. Meanwhile I am recognised as an "Autism specialist" in another school and have also become quite involved with the Autistic Society. I keep savouring the silence of my little cottage and the grandeur of the mountains, which I still tend to climb a lot faster than the guidebooks suggest. I am about to play my cello again in church, and I go everywhere on my bicycle, rain or shine, floods or snow, as I have never mastered driving a car. I can relate to children whom others deem to be unreachable, yet I find it hard to relate to most adults. Yes, I am different from the "norm", but I can accept it better now that I know where it stems from.

Recently I have been offered a new form of psychotherapy, called Eye Movement Desensitization and Reprocessing (EMDR), which uses sensory stimuli to act directly on the emotional or limbic brain. Followed up with sessions of video and social skills therapy, it has given me new hope of overcoming anxiety and depression and of replacing my profound loneliness with meaningful relationships. Coming to know other people with Asperger Syndrome has also been a great help, like meeting someone who speaks your own language in a foreign land and culture.

In front of me I have got a little box I made in a workshop on the Isle of Iona, which displays different aspects of my life. The four sides say: God's child, teacher, mountaineer and author. The bottom is brown, earthy brown, my favourite colour beside navy blue. The lid shows an elk, the symbol for my name, and the words: "Free to open". Inside is a little foam dog who looks like Matthew, and there are other beautiful images and a not so beautiful black whirlwind. All this is part of me, part of who I am, and all the different aspects are related to each other and interwoven with a world view shaped by Asperger Syndrome. I am still excited to have found the underlying cause of my problems, yet this will not stop me from going on to discover more of who I am, just as it doesn't solve my daily struggle with life. I hope that by sharing my story others may be encouraged to discover more about themselves and enhance their understanding of those with whom they live or work.

Epilogue

For the past thirty years, the diagnosis of Autism Spectrum Disorders (ASD) has been based on the Triad of Impairments, i.e. repetitive, stereotyped patterns of behaviour and difficulties in social communication and social interaction. The treatment which followed is mainly concentrating on modifying behaviour and facilitating social communication and interaction. What most professionals, despite research evidence and testimonies of people with ASD, fail to take sufficient account of are the sensory issues which, I would argue, underlie all behaviour.

Hearing a wider range of frequencies than what is considered normal for humans makes it extremely difficult to pick up the nuances of verbal language. The confusion created by visual over stimulation can lead to closing out part of the picture, while fixing the gaze on a particular detail. Having a stronger sense of smell and a greater sensitivity to tactile influence on the skin might be responsible for the fear of touch or of closeness to other people. The stress felt by the bewildering amount of sensory input may then lead to the withdrawal into oneself, the stereotypical repetitive behaviours and the difficulty in understanding the world and other people, therefore responding to them in inappropriate ways.

Instead of the diagnostic triangle, this would be a linear approach of cause and effect. It is widely agreed that an abnormality in the brain is responsible for ASD, but if hypersensitivity or a different way of processing sensory stimuli was to be seen as underlying all other problems associated with Autism and Asperger Syndrome, the consequences for treatment and education (and most of all for living conditions) would be enormous.

I am currently studying for a Postgraduate Diploma in Inclusive Practice (formerly called Remedial or Special Needs Education). The present trend in education is to include every child in their local mainstream school, catering for diverse needs by adapting the physical environment, the curriculum and teaching styles to give everybody the highest quality learning experience, while keeping them all under one roof. Although the intention is excellent and has led to many innovative initiatives, teaching staff struggle immensely in trying to make it work.

One group of children for whom this system creates the greatest difficulties are those on the Autistic Spectrum, including Asperger Syndrome. It is the very inclusiveness of different learning styles – academic and practical, individual and group based, rote learning and experimental – at one time in one class room which excludes these children, as the bewildering amount of what is going on around them overloads their sensory system. A busy class room with various groups of children working in different ways on different tasks is felt as chaos, and in an attempt to restore order, the child will either withdraw or hit out (flight or fight as reaction to stress). For a hypersensitive child, to achieve the highest possible learning experience (or in some cases simply to learn at all) is only possible in a calm and orderly environment.

Also, as a teacher I have never seen a child on the Autistic Spectrum being socially included in a mainstream class room, neither did I experience this as a child. Yet whilst helping with the Highland Autistic Playscheeme Initiative during the summer holidays, I was astonished to see these same children play happily with one another, obviously linked by a common bond of understanding and interests. Just as a piece of jigsaw puzzle only fits into the picture from which it was taken, so we all need to find our particular groups of people to whom we feel a sense of belonging.

This does not end when we leave the education system, just as Autism and Asperger Syndrome do not end when we grow up. I was very fortunate to have relatives, friends and Christian establishments that offered me a place to work and to live while I was not yet ready to cope on my own in the "big world", but a lot of vulnerable people are not so fortunate. We desperately need more sheltered communities to include people for whom inclusion in mainstream society does not work. As we are building more and more nursing homes for old people and day nurseries for babies and infants, why is it so hard to acknowledge that there are other groups of people in our society who need a more sheltered environment in order to have a fulfilling life?

And finally, since hypersensitivity is the most important aspect of Autism Spectrum Disorders, perhaps the fact that our homes, streets and workplaces have become so full of electronic noise, bright visual stimuli and crowded with smells from all around the world, has something to do with the high increase of ASD. Of course, more research would have to be done to come to a definite conclusion. In the meantime, I hope to have made some contribution to the understanding of people on the Spectrum and of our needs and strengths.

Recommended Reading:

Andron, Linda (ed.), (2001). *Our Journey through High Functioning Autism & Asperger Syndrome,* London: Jessica Kingsley Publ.

Attwood, Tony, (2001). *Asperger Syndrome,* London: Jessica Kingsley Publ.

Bogdashina, Olga, (2003). *Sensory Perceptual Issues in Autism,* London: Jessica Kingsley Publ.

Frith, Uta, (2003). *Autism: Explaining the enigma,* Oxford: Blackwell Publ.

Gillberg, Christopher, (2002). *A Guide to Asperger Syndrome,* Cambridge University Press.

Grandin, Temple, (1995). *Thinking in Pictures,* New York: Vintage Books.

Mont, Daniel, (2002). *A Different kind of Boy,* London: Jessica Kingsley Publ.

Sainsbury, Clare, (2000). *Martian in the Playground,* Bristol: Lucky Duck Publ.

Williams, Donna, (1998). *Autism and Sensing,* London: Jessica Kingsley Publ.

Zelan, Karen, (2003). *Between their world and ours,* New York: St. Martin's Press.

Useful Websites:

The National Autistic Society
www.autism.org.uk

The Scottish Society for Autism
www.autism-in-scotland.org.uk

Others
http://www.udel.edu/bkirby/asperger/index.html

http://autism.simplenet.com/